Maclean Press, Isle of Skye

THE SUMMER OF '89

Being the Photographic Record
of a Scottish Highland Summer Tour
in the year 1889 by an English
Gentleman from Tunbridge Wells

by
Bob Charnley

Skye & Lochalsh District Council's
Museums Service

© Text, Bob Charnley, 1991

© Photographs, The Bob Charnley Collection 1991 unless otherwise credited

Period Equipment, Museum of Science & Engineering, Newcastle upon Tyne
(Tyne & Wear Museums)

Designed and Produced by Design Publicity Ltd, Newcastle upon Tyne,
Printed in England for the Publishers...

Maclean Press. 60 Aird Bhearnasdail, by Portree, Isle of Skye. Tel: 047 032 309

British Library Cataloguing in Publication Data
Charnley, Bob
The Summer of '89

ISBN: 0 9516022 1 7

DEDICATION

This book is dedicated to a little boy named Calum from Quarry, Glenelg, who was born in April 1989 to Donna and Eddie Stiven. Exactly one hundred years earlier, in April 1889, a baby boy named Solomon was born to Isabella and Alexander MacDonald, travelling tinsmiths.

Isabella MacDonald is the beautiful woman on the cover of this book. In August 1889, whilst carrying Solomon on her back, she was photographed outside a croft in Quarry, Glenelg. This is the exact site of Calum's home today.

May Calum have a happy childhood! And to his loving parents I send my very sincere thanks for all the help they have given to me during the last four years.

ABOUT THE AUTHOR

Bob Charnley was born in Lancashire in 1940 and educated at Stonyhurst College and St. Augustine's College, Co.Cavan. After a period of employment with the food giant H.J. Heinz & Co. Ltd. at Kitt Green, Wigan and Harlesden, London, in the early 1960s, he joined the Metropolitan Police.

As a young officer he served in prestigious 'A' Division stationed at Rochester Row and the Palace of Westminster, and in his first few years he attended at such varied events as the Lying in State of Sir Winston Churchill and the violent affair in front of the United States Embassy in Grosvenor Square, when a small force of officers came under intense attack from an overwhelming number of demonstrators. He is clearly visible on those old black and white film clips of the sixties if you know where to look!

In the 1970s he served as a CID officer with Lancashire Constabulary in a highly specialized role. At this time he met and married his wife Sandra, daughter of a fellow officer, and they continue to live in that county.

Bob's present collection of photographs, postcards, books and ephemera from the Scottish Highlands and Islands numbers in excess of 5,000 items and includes an unpublished typescript of a 1913 journey to the remote island of St. Kilda, and a recently discovered collection of photos taken on that island in 1901.

He now enjoys frequent visits to the Highlands and Outer Hebrides between periods acting as a consultant on art and antiques to the Samlesbury Hall Trust at their fourteenth century manor house near Blackburn in Lancashire.

ACKNOWLEDGEMENTS

To many people I owe a great deal for their involvement in my travels over the last few years, but to Anne Hurst of Manchester I am particularly indebted. Anne is responsible for my guardianship of the **Scotch Tour 1889** album today and without her this book might never have been written.

My friend Michael Day of Little Sutton, Wirral, has seen more of the original photographs than any other person for he has studied, copied and enlarged most of the images in the album over the last five years. The proof of his great skill and care with the pictures can be seen within these pages.

The triumvirate of Doctors, Kenneth Gibson, Alan Marchbank and Ann Matheson, together with Jackie Cromarty at the National Library of Scotland in Edinburgh, have been kindness personified and their professional advice has been of the greatest help to this particular Englishman.

That stalwart of the Highland Folk Museum at Kingussie, curator Ross Noble, together with Helen Collie and all the team members, has been a keen supporter of the album and our quest in following the path of the original photographer. May their ventures at Kingussie and Newtonmore bring them more success over the next few years.

In our travels along the 'Scotch Tour' route from Edinburgh to Inverness, through Perthshire and from Aultbea through Gairloch to Balmacara, ending in Oban, Sandra and I have been assisted by many people in all these towns and villages and their collective hospitality has ensured a pleasant passage for us both.

In the villages of Letterfearn and Glenelg we received a most considerable amount of help which will be evident from the details given in text and captions. Grandchildren and great-grandchildren of the 1889 villagers continue to live in both places and they passed on their knowledge generously. We cannot over-emphasis our gratitude to all of them.

Particularly I would single out Margaret MacPherson in Glenelg. We first met, under unusual circumstances, at the Highland Trade Fair in Aviemore and have kept in touch ever since. When Margaret has not been in Italy she has opened doors for me in Glenelg! I am delighted to be able to show a photograph of her great-grandmother as she looked in 1889.

We had the very great good fortune to meet Donna Dimambro and Eddie Stiven in 1986. Now, as Mr. and Mrs. Stiven, they continue as our good friends, and we are immensely grateful for everything they have done for us. Their connection with the album will be evident from the text and the dedication of this book to their lovely son Calum.

To the Skye and Lochalsh District Council Museum's Service Officer in Portree, Roger Miket, I can only apologize for all the things I have asked him to do for me over the last four years. He never let me down but I have kept him waiting for this book longer than anticipated. There was always a tomorrow!

ACKNOWLEDGEMENTS

I am consoled in the knowledge that the composer Manuel de Falla planned his 'Nights in the Gardens of Spain' as a solo piece for pianoforte in the early 1900's but it took around ten years to complete and emerged as a piece for orchestra and piano.

Roger must be pleased I cannot compose music!

Along the way in England, from Combe Hay to Tunbridge Wells and Scarborough, I have met and been guided by many people too numerous to mention, but they have my thanks for all the help they offered. The photographs are the work of Francis Smart and the words are mine, but I am very grateful to former Mail and Daily Mirror journalist Reg White who gave up some of his precious retirement time to read, encourage and correct my literary effort.

And finally, to Sandra I send my love. She has lived more without than with me during many frequent trips to Scotland and elsewhere, but we have also enjoyed a few more pleasant holidays together in the Highlands since the album came into our guardianship. We have visited many different Highland villages together and met new people who are now our friends. It has been fun! Thank-you all!

CONTENTS

CHAPTER ONE
A·M·D·G
The Album Discovered!

It was the face of that Tinker Woman gazing proudly from the faded sepia photograph in the scuffed album that started it all. The powerful image of the hauntingly-beautiful woman of indeterminate age, her wares looped over her arm, a baby slung on her back, had a devastating impact on me.

As I leafed through the album, in a second-hand bookshop in Cheshire, it became apparent that the photographs were a private record of a holiday taken during the summer months of 1889. The 283 photographs were of some places I had never heard of in the Scottish Highlands and unnamed people photographed by an unknown traveller.

As an avid collector of photographs, books, postcards and ephemera of The Highlands and Islands I was, to say the least, intrigued by the album.

The photographer, working with what we would now regard as antique cameras, undoubtedly knew his craft. He had a natural eye for a good picture and had gone off the beaten track in search of subjects. In doing so he had left behind a unique record of work, play and interests of the Highlanders of the nineteenth century, their villages and their homes.

Yet although he had spent a considerable amount of money on the leather-bound album, with *'Scotch Tour 1889'* engraved in gold lettering on the cover and spine, he had not included his name or book-plate within the covers.

I must declare now that, as a former detective, I have an in-built curiosity and thirst for facts, which no doubt inspired the urge to find out the identity of that intrepid photographer who journeyed through the Highlands a century ago. Equally, I had to see some of those unknown villages and perhaps put names to a few faces.

My wife, Sandra, and I did not realize then that the quest was to take over our lives for the next five years!

Collecting has always been a personal passion of mine.

Like many children before me and since I, too, had my little stamp album with imperfect copies of Victorian 1d Reds, and even a 2d Blue, alongside the bigger stamps from the various exhibitions, silver weddings and festivals of the first 50 years of this century. But in 1949 I was packed off to a preparatory school, lost all interest in my stamps and learnt the art of photography from a Jesuit priest dedicated to the teaching of small gentlemen.

The mysteries of the camera and the darkroom came slowly but Father O'Neil, a great enthusiast with the camera, persevered and within a term or two I was capable of developing and printing my own films and all before the age of ten.

The knowledge gained in those early days was put to good use a decade later when I joined the staff of H.J. Heinz at their show-piece factory at Kitt Green near Wigan. I was given my very own darkroom and let loose on the factory floor with a camera and flash gun.

For a few years everything went well until one afternoon a large flash bulb blew up whilst I was taking a photograph of canning machinery on a soup line. It was feared that small fragments of glass might have reached the product so the whole batch was thrown away. Perhaps that is why the management offered me a job 200 miles south at their factory in Harlesden. But I ended up as a London policeman instead! The daily factory routine was not for me and I decided to desert the baked beans for the smart blue serge.

It was 1964 and, as everyone now knows, London was swinging. They were great days! I was young, single and living in police accommodation in prestigious Ambrosden Avenue, just 100 yards away from Westminster Cathedral and close to my place of work

The Album

at Rochester Row Police Station. The shift system allowed me time to roam the antique markets of the capital. My collecting years were about to begin in earnest.

Roman coins came first followed by pottery jugs and plates made in the 1820s in Staffordshire. In the early seventies, and now married, I started a collection of British Cigarette Cards and then came my current interest in Victorian and Edwardian photographs, postcards, books and ephemera of the Scottish Highlands and Islands.

It was a dry, cold January day in 1986 and we were in Cheshire, savouring a day out and calling at second-hand book shops in the towns and villages we passed through. At this particular time there was an antiquarian bookshop in the very centre of Stockport and we could usually rely on the lady, who looked after the shop for the owner, to have found some interesting, early Scottish postcards that could be added to the collection. We drew a blank with the postcards but from a miscellaneous assortment of books the lady produced a dusty and slightly scuffed, leather bound album.

'This might interest you!' she said confidently as she handed it to me.

The album, with *'Scotch Tour 1889'* in gold lettering on the spine and cover, looked interesting enough. It was packed with sepia images of people and some places in the Highlands that I had never heard of. I sat down at a table and thumbed through the pages.

'It's a bit disappointing,' I said after a while; really to no one in particular.

'What do you mean?' enquired the lady.

'Well I was hoping he might have gone out to the islands and taken some photographs but I can only find one of Portree on the Isle of Skye,' I moaned. Quick as a flash she came back at me.

'Yes but he took plenty in Oban and you have a big collection of that town haven't you?' A lady with a good memory, I thought.

It was true that my collection of the town exceeded one thousand items at this time, most dating from the early 1900s, and the few Victorian images were mostly commercial views taken by such people as George Washington Wilson, Photographer Royal in Scotland, or Argyll based McIsaac and Riddle, who sold their pictures over the bookshop counter to intrepid tourists who did not own cameras.

But the album in my hands that day was different. The pictures were unique, individual in style, and they showed Highlanders going about their business or letting their hair down. A far cry from the commercially-aimed shots of Princes Street. I had another moan.

'The back of the album is full of pictures of Combe Hay, wherever that is, and they don't look very Scottish to me!'

The lady looked over my shoulder and agreed. Neither of us had heard of Combe Hay.

'What do you think?' she asked hopefully. 'Is it any use to you?'

I mumbled into my beard and turned back towards the centre pages of the album where something had caught my eye.

'Yes, I am interested if we can agree a price,' I muttered, trying to hide my excitement, for I had caught sight of that superb photograph of a young woman, with a baby on her back, carrying her pans and pails *(98)*.

I studied it for a few seconds, snapped the album shut and stood up.

'How much?' I ventured.

A figure was mentioned and I recoiled. It was too much!

There followed an amount of good-humoured bargaining that is normal practice on such occasions, and the price came down by ten per cent. Finally it was rounded down to the nearest multiple of ten and it was all over.

We were both winners. I owned the album and had paid less than the asking price. The bookshop owner had his profit and the chance to buy more stock. Sandra however was a little less enthusiastic about the whole deal.

'Haven't you got enough photos of Oban already?' she grumbled.

'Yes, but there are pictures from other places apart from Oban,' I replied defensively.

Two days later we had a chance to sit down together and go through the album page by page and examine all 283 photographs.

Slowly we turned each page examining the sepia prints which vary in size from 6 x 4.5 down to 4 x 3 inches. Sandra was now beginning to share my excitement.

'I still think this is the best,' I said, as I looked at that Tinker Woman again.

Sandra stood up, left the room, and returned moments later with a folding pocket magnifying glass from her handbag, an essential item for collectors.

'Turn back to the tinker camp picture again,' she said. 'I think the little girl standing next to the woman is in the photo taken at the camp' *(76)*.

I felt like Sherlock Holmes, magnifying glass in hand with Watson by my side, and I smiled as I recalled that Sir Arthur Conan Doyle, Holmes's creator, had been a pupil at my old school, Stonyhurst College in Lancashire, although a good few generations earlier!

I studied the picture of the camp with a young girl staring from behind the canvas, smiling at the photographer. She wore a distinctive double buckle belt and was, indeed, the same child photographed next to that Tinker Woman at Glenelg, a small Highland village on the mainland opposite the Isle of Skye.

Our unknown traveller, it seemed, had started at Carlisle and worked his way up through the Border towns of Melrose and Jedburgh before passing on to Edinburgh. From the capital he moved north to Dunkeld, Pitlochry and district and then up to the coast at Nairn and Inverness before turning west towards Aultbea and Gairloch. Then south by sea to Letterfearn, Glenelg and Oban, visiting Dalmally and Inveraray before returning to Edinburgh and Combe Hay, which we now know to be a small village some four miles south-west of Bath.

'Good job he captioned everything or we would never have known where he had been,' laughed Sandra.

I had to agree, for beneath each photograph or at the top of the page was a handwritten location or brief comment such as *"Poolewe"* or *"view from our window"*.

Little did we realize how valuable these clues would be in the years ahead.

'What a great picture of an old fisherman!' I said, pointing to a fine study captioned simply *'Nairn'. (38)* And a few minutes later:

'Just look at these children at Letterfearn!' I exclaimed. 'This man really knew something about photography. See how he composed this group!' *(66)*.

That night we sat for hours, enraptured by the artistry of that pioneering photographer who had brought to life wonderful cameos of the Highlands of a century ago. We were captivated by the scenes of ordinary people going about their daily tasks, children collecting whelks on the shore at Aultbea *(46)*, and the group watching the fisherman in Nairn with his nets. *(38)* A road repairer near Pitlochry *(24)*, and an old lady knitting contentedly somewhere near Blair Atholl. *(32)* Women doing the washing *(33)*, men competing in a sack race *(93)*, hammer-throwers *(87)* and dancers *(91)* at the Glenelg Games, and yachts under full canvas in Oban bay. *(111)* So many vivid images!

There was no doubt in my mind that we had discovered an important collection of valuable photographs. Their existence was obviously unknown, otherwise the images would have been reproduced many times in the 'Victorian Scotland' publications that are so popular north of the Border. But our excitement was tinged with disappointment.

'If only the photographer had put his name in the front of the album,' I sighed. 'I really would like to know who he was!' That was wishful thinking late into the night. We put the album away and went to bed.

About a week later I went back to the bookshop, confident of answers to a list of questions I had prepared. My friendly seller was at the counter.

'Did you buy the old photograph album at an auction or from the family?' I enquired politely.

'No, it came from a runner,' she replied. Ah! Not the answer I had expected!

Runners are useful people; some are retired gentlefolk but most are persons who buy items in one part of the country and sell elsewhere for a living. Usually they find a dealer many miles away who has a client for what they are offering to sell. There is nothing shady about the business (well not in most cases) but confidentiality rules and I drew the proverbial blank! I did discover that the runner in question came from the West Country but I know no more than that. Should you know anything about the history of the album in this century please do let me know!

So, just who was the photographer? What part of the United Kingdom did he come from and what camera did he use? Was he famous or just an unknown gifted amateur and who had owned the album for the last fifty years or so?

All these were the usual questions a detective might ask and expect to receive the answers to, but in this case we had no known witnesses, just the album, and it contained precious few clues.

There was a style about the photographer; a feeling that he wanted to compose his subject not just 'point and shoot'. He may have photographed everything he saw but the album surely must hold the pictures that gave him, and his family, the greatest pleasure and sense of achievement after the journey was over. After all, each picture had been pasted into the album and captioned, however briefly, and then the album had been taken to a local bookbinder who gold-tooled the front cover and spine so that it was worthy of a place on a Victorian gentleman's library shelf. He had every right to be proud of it.

The picture of that Tinker Woman, so simply dressed yet almost elegant, was to make quite an impression subsequently. I have even heard her compared to the Mona Lisa!

In 1988 at the Iona Gallery in the Highland Folk Museum, Kingussie, during an exhibition of some fifty enlarged pictures from the album, I met a group of Members of the European Parliament from the continent who called in during a fact-finding tour. The one photograph they all wanted to talk about and look at was this picture of the Tinker Woman, indeed it was difficult to persuade the Spanish MEP in the group that the lady was not from his country. He repeatedly asked if it was certain that the picture was taken in Scotland and even when he conceded that point he still argued that she originally must have come from Spain!

The winter months of 1986 gradually gave way to warmer weather and I made a small and relatively insignificant decision, little realising then how it would alter our lives.

'How about a few days in Scotland at Easter?' I asked Sandra. 'We could go and look at some of the places in the album and see how much they have changed since 1889.'

She readily agreed and that is how we embarked on a quest with no guide to direct us other than the images themselves.

I hoped the photographs might allow us to reach back to that vanished world and recover something of the people and places captured by our mysterious Victorian photographer. As the majority of his photographs were concentrated on Kintail, Letterfearn and Glenelg in Ross-shire and Inverness-shire, we decided to follow our unknown traveller and make this our first destination.

I had no inkling then that I would cover some 80,000 miles throughout Scotland and the South of England before the case of the Victorian photographer was finally solved.

CHAPTER TWO

The Quest Begins

'Just look at the snow on those mountains,' exclaimed Sandra. 'Isn't this a beautiful place!'

It was the week before Easter and we were driving along the A87 road approaching Glen Shiel. In 1719, a combined force of Spaniards and Jacobites had met and fought against Government soldiers at this place, and brief visions of that skirmish flashed across my mind as we neared the bridge where it all took place. But the snow-dusted summits of the Five Sisters of Kintail proved a greater distraction. The view really was quite magnificent and we were looking forward to this short break with some enthusiasm.

I had read a few books, written in the Thirties and late 1940s, about the district we were about to visit, but the area around Glen Shiel and Kintail was really unfamiliar ground to us when we left home for Kyle of Lochalsh. We had chosen Kyle because it appeared to be a good base for visiting Balmacara, Letterfearn and Glenelg, yet it still gave access to the needs of the twentieth century visitor, such as banks, a main post office, railway station and a greater range of accommodation.

From our hotel in Kyle, that week, we 'discovered' what thousands were already aware of; the great majesty of Kintail. And whilst the coaches dashed past from Fort William, crowded with fellow Lancastrians on their half day tour of Skye, we took a stroll around the shores of Loch Duich trying to find the exact spots from which the photographs had been taken.

The road from Shiel Bridge through Ratagan to Letterfearn is good but narrow and initially every turn in the road looked just like one from a photo in the album. Yes, the trees were bigger and some of the 1889 stone walls may have gone but this was just how our Victorian photographer would have seen it, if one could ignore the twentieth century fish farm cages on the loch, the telephone box and the motor car!

Although Letterfearn was quiet that day, it was impossible to be unaware of the passing glances from the few local people going about their daily routine. There was this bearded Englishman, 6'3", 15 stone and with a quizzical look, trying to appear inconspicuous and it really was not working!

Who would not be suspicious of someone walking around with a big book, looking at their house and garden, making notes and taking photographs. What new motorway route was being planned for the village, or which council department was he from?

In the end we decided to look for help, for if anyone could assist in locating the sites of the 1889 photographs it would be someone whose home was in the village. A car pulled up close to where we were standing and the driver got out. He looked friendly and we walked towards him.

'Excuse me,' I said, 'but do you know exactly where this picture was taken from?' I offered him a black and white print which showed boats moored by the shore with people in and around them. *(63)* The word *'Letterfearn'* was the simple caption on the album page.

He took it from me, studied it for the briefest of moments and handed it back, his face beaming.

'I keep a boat there myself!' he exclaimed. 'But when was this picture taken?'

'Oh, 1889,' I said boastfully. 'Would you like to see some more?'

And so Donald Campbell of Letterfearn became the first person, since 1889, to see the photographs of his village with the neat thatching and the beautiful children.

He was immensely helpful and within half an hour the exact site of many of the

Shiel Bridge in 1860.

pictures had been discovered. But more than that, Donald provided the name and address of someone in Glenelg, a few miles away over Mam Ratagan (Rattachan or Rattagan as the Victorians spelt it in 1889) who might be able to provide further information.

Mam Ratagan is that *'terrible steep to climb'* mountain that stood in the way of Samuel Johnson and James Boswell in September, 1773, on their journey through Glenelg to the Hebrides.

A century later a gentleman named George Birkbeck Hill wrote *'Footsteps of Dr. Johnson'* during the spring and summer months of 1889 and on 21 June, just a few weeks before a fellow traveller with his camera was to arrive, he was in Glenelg. This is his contemporary description of the area:

> *'At the most delightful time of the year, when the days were at their longest and no candles were burnt, there was scarcely a single stranger to enjoy the quiet and the beauty. There were woods and flowering shrubs, rhododendrons and the Portugal laurel, and close to the water's edge the laburnum in full bloom. There were all the sights of peaceful country life-the cocks crowing, the sheep answering with their bleats their bleating lambs, the cows with their calves in the noonday heat seeking the shade of the tall and wide-spreading trees. The waves lapped gently on the shore, and in the distance, below the rocky coast of Skye, the waters were whitened by the countless sea-birds. We drove up a beautiful valley to the Pictish forts, and saw an eagle hovering high above us.'*

Though unknown to us at the time, our 1986 trip to Glenelg was to be the first of many; by December, 1990, I had crossed the mountain for the fiftieth time.

Donald Campbell had given us the name and address of Duncan Cameron, but when we found his house we discovered he was out at work in the forest and would not be back until later in the day. We decided to do some exploring on our own.

The Victorian traveller approached Glenelg from the sea on board one of David MacBrayne's paddle steamers and he is to be envied his route. That mode of transport is no longer available from Oban today. But the water is always with you in Glenelg and the differing moods and reflections cast a spell over the visitor. A change of direction, as you drive towards the old ferry house at the crossing place for Skye, and the village looks quite different.

How our anonymous photographer must have enjoyed the light of those August days in 1889. Records show that the weather was sunny and dry, and consequently his time exposures were shortened, his depth of field greater, and he was guaranteed pin-sharp pictures every time on his large glass negatives.

A modern 35 mm camera, plus a great array of lenses, gives a similar guarantee but the end results are never quite the same somehow! No doubt about it, the negative size is the culprit and a small negative, however well exposed, will never better the larger size.

Without knowing how my pictures would turn out I decided, then and there, to put the equipment away and concentrate on physically finding the 1889 sites. We already had a collection of great photographs and I was not the person to better them.

Walking around Glenelg that day was just as exciting as arriving in some foreign country for the first time. We both had a sense of adventure and, in my case, a feeling that here in this village, there was some historical detective work to do.

The analogy with a murder case was to be made later, in 1989, by a journalist with a Scottish publication. A bit gruesome, I thought, but he likened the Stockport bookshop to the murder scene and the album to the body! He had already placed me, as a former detective in the Lancashire Constabulary, as the investigating officer who was out to get his man. It was an interesting piece of writing and I had to smile, but I would never have called the photographer a suspect.

Certainly there was a determination to put a few names to faces and locations but the only criticism that could be levelled at the photographer was that he failed to inscribe his own name and address in the front of the album.

Now that's what a detective really likes; the suspect leaving his business card at the scene of the crime, but perhaps he had left just one small fingerprint somewhere for us to find!

When television personality Anneka Rice visited Glenelg, on one of her *'Treasure Hunt'* missions, it was in a helicopter speeding across the water from Skye at wave height. As her pilot banked and climbed to 1000 feet the viewer caught a glimpse of the whole magnificent area. Protected by the sea to the west, and by hills everywhere else, Glenelg sits at the end of a lush, fertile valley.

Once it had all been the property of the MacLeods of MacLeod, Chieftains of Dunvegan Castle on Skye, but in 1811 the 24th Chief, John Norman, sold out, and the area continued to be bought and sold until 1837 when a Mr. James Baillie paid in excess of £75,000 for it. He lived in Dochfour, a beautifully wooded area five miles south west of Inverness, where he had built a Venetian-style mansion, described as *'new and very elegant, with a fine garden'* by His Royal Highness Prince Albert when he visited the area in September, 1847.

Two years later, in 1849 (forty years before the photographs were taken), Mr. Baillie assisted over 500 residents of Glenelg to emigrate to Canada. He generously provided

£2,000 from his own pocket with a further £500 added by the Highland Destitution Committee.

What an opportunity for the villagers! Entirely voluntarily they boarded the sailing ship *'Liscard'* bound for Quebec, their food and passage paid for, warm clothing provided for the less fortunate, plus a cash allowance to cover their needs for a period of one month on arrival. So popular was the offer that it became over-subscribed and a further fifty families missed the boat. Unfortunately this group had already sold all their possessions and were stranded on the shores of Loch Hourn, miles from Glenelg, with little food and even less shelter.

However the gesture made by Mr. Baillie was *not* generous. In effect he bought his way out of a problem offering the *'frying-pan or the fire'* to the people. They were merely small tenants on his estate and considerably less productive than a rich, individual tenant who could afford to put thousands of sheep into the fields and hills of Glenelg. The *'generous'* offer of free emigration was a last resort both for himself and for the people. If they declined to leave then a rent increase would probably have the same desired effect.

But most of all, the people did not own the land they worked, and the sting in the tail was that they had to agree to pull down their croft-houses, or huts, in Glenelg before setting off for the ship and their *'free passage'*. There was no turning back.

The unfortunates who missed the boat and wandered, starving, around Loch Hourn were asked if they were still willing to emigrate.

'With one voice they assured me', wrote Thomas Mulock, editor of the *'Inverness Advertiser'*, *'that nothing short of the impossibility of obtaining land or employment at home could drive them to seek the doubtful benefits of a foreign shore.'*

Years later Alexander MacKenzie, writing in his 1883 book about the Highland Clearances, summed up the dreadful episode in this one sentence:

'If a judicious system had been applied of cultivating excellent land, capable of producing food in abundance in Glenelg, there was not another property in the Highlands on which it was less necessary to send people away than in that beautiful and fertile valley.'

A few hours after our arrival in Glenelg it was lunch-time, so we did what most visitors would do and went to the Glenelg Inn, the only hotel in the village. The bar seemed surprisingly empty when we arrived.

Now from Easter Saturday, until a date which varies from mid-September to the end of October, everything is open in Scotland; hotels, guest houses, tourist information offices, restaurants, cafes and inns. But if you arrive in some places just a few days early you will be unlucky. The tourist office will be closed, the paint still wet in the guest-house bedrooms and there will be nowhere to eat until Saturday morning. Visitors are really not catered for in some Highland places, before Easter. We had arrived in Glenelg on Maundy Thursday and lunch was a packet of crisps with the drink having to come from a barrel or the bottle!

We decided to take the direct approach and show the pictures to the man behind the bar.

'That's this place before it burnt down.' confirmed the barman as he selected one of the pictures. He turned out to be the youthful owner, Christopher Main.

'We have this picture on the wall over there,' he said, pointing in the direction of the pool table. I walked across the room.

'He can't have!' I muttered under my breath, as I gazed on a collection of old sepia photographs on the wall. And I was right, he didn't have *this* one! *(82)*

My 1889 photograph shows the Glenelg Hotel, and the pictures on the walls were indeed of the same building but they were copies of commercial prints produced by the Aberdeen company of George Washington Wilson, and others, in the 1870s and eighties. Sadly the fine building was destroyed by fire during the winter of 1947.

I showed Christopher some more pictures and within 30 minutes, with a couple of phone calls, he had increased the number of customers threefold.

Most came out of curiosity but a few spent some time searching for their own homes on the photographs. Others hoped to recognize a face in the crowd despite the fact that the pictures were almost a century old at this time.

A few tentative identifications were suggested but the most important part of that particular day was that we met and talked with people of the village.

Over the next few hours we listened to stories from the past told by people whose parents, grand-parents or great grand-parents were alive and living in the village in 1889. The album was a link with the past and the photographs of the area were being seen, for the first time in the village, almost 100 years after they had been taken.

It was an exciting day and our short stay in the district was a great success!

Back at home I took the opportunity to check my dossier and evaluate all the little bits of information we had gathered. In Glenelg, for example, there were people old enough to have known some of the people whose photographs appeared in the album and indeed

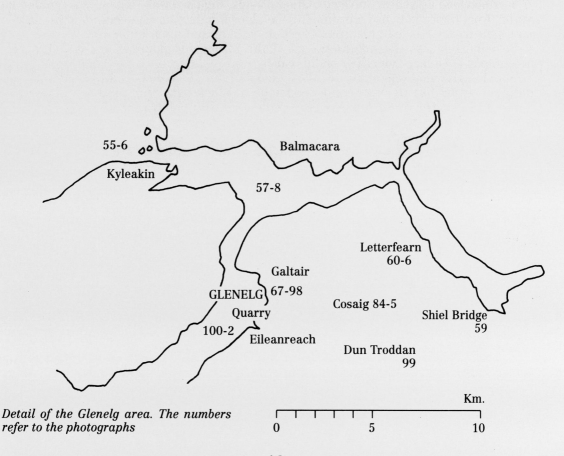

Detail of the Glenelg area. The numbers refer to the photographs

some names had been suggested for a face or two. I was hooked and within a few weeks I was back in the village, alone this time, looking for more clues.

It was a warm summer day when I finally managed to meet up with Duncan Cameron, the crofter/forester Donald Campbell had advised me to seek out. Covered with sawdust and twigs this figure emerged from the forest on the slopes of Mam Ratagan and I introduced myself.

'Yes, I've heard about these photographs,' Duncan said, staring at me intently. 'Come around to the house and let me have a look through them.'

Duncan is a man with a strong physical presence coupled with a great sharpness of mind, and I remember thinking that I could have done with him alongside me during my early years with the Metropolitan Police. Four years later Duncan and I were sat in the bar at the Castle Inn in Dornie, enjoying a good lunch and a Christmas drink, chatting about the clearances from Skye and Glenelg in those far off days, when the conversation switched to his own ancestors and their links with the constabulary. Duncan told me that his grandfather, Ewen Cameron, was present at the 'Battle of the Braes', on the Isle of Skye, in April 1882 as a young police constable, and Ewen's son (Duncan's father) also joined the constabulary. The Cameron line remains unbroken to this day with Duncan's brother serving as a senior police officer in Aberdeen.

Initially I think Duncan was a bit suspicious of me but the album broke down any barriers between us and we have remained friends. In fact it was Duncan who guided me around, from house to house, introducing the older inhabitants especially, and he showed great patience as I asked numerous questions of him and his friends. Hours were spent as the village elders turned the pages of the album for themselves, searching the photographs for a face from their childhood.

Sadly I regret that one or two of those people have since died and to their surviving relatives I would like to express my condolences. I look back with especial fondness on my visit to John *'The Gaffy'* MacAskill, a gentle man with plenty of stories of earlier days and a good memory for faces; his help was invaluable when it came to putting names to faces and he is sadly missed.

Late one afternoon I went for a short walk away from the centre of the village and along the shore to the south. Few people were about, and as I passed the impressive war memorial, and the scattered houses with their uninterrupted view of Skye, I spotted a sign by the front gate of a small bungalow. *'Glenelg Candles'* it read. I decided to pay a visit, and in the workshop at the rear of the premises I found a young woman at a bench doing creative things with molten wax, the sun shining on the incredible mass of her auburn hair, a radio playing in the background.

This was my first sight of Donna Dimambro.

We struck up a conversation and I told her about the photographs and of my search for names, sites and, hopefully, the identity of the photographer. Donna said she might be able to help with some of the locations but as my time was limited that afternoon I promised to return with the album the next day.

Away from Glenelg and over Mam Ratagan lies Aultachruine, a small hamlet off the busy road to Kyle of Lochalsh, and it was to here that I returned each evening; my base being a comfortable bed and breakfast establishment, called *Tigh-na-Mara,* chosen at random from the local tourist guide.

My host turned out to be a great local character, Yunnie Mackinnon, a generous extrovert who could probably give the lawyers of Aberdeen a good run for their money. Her wholehearted optimism for life is tempered by Iain her husband, a true, soft spoken Highland gentleman, whose daily needs in life are simple. He has the magnificence of the mountains of Kintail on his doorstep and a loch full of fish at the bottom of the croft. Life is not to be rushed in such idyllic surroundings!

I would join Yunnie and Iain each evening around the dining table and make my daily report over the fish course! Yunnie would then tell me where I had gone wrong, the name of the person I *should* have visited in a particular village and someone I *must* see immediately! She would then pick up her much-used phone and issue the summonses.

The court was in session and attendance was mandatory, and a succession of wonderful people came through the patio window every night to look at the album!

But a regular highlight of my stay would be the visits to the Clachan Bar at Dornie, close to the famed castle of Eilean Donan.

Our unknown traveller never photographed this castle for the simplest of reasons; Eilean Donan Castle in 1889 was derelict, having been virtually destroyed in 1719 by the heavy guns of His Majesty's Ships *'Worcester'* and *'Enterprise'*. What you see today is a highly photogenic creation of the twentieth century, having been completed in the early Thirties. For all that it is familiar to people the world over, appears on biscuit and chocolate box tops and is a tremendous tourist asset for Scotland.

But back to the inn at Dornie; and here I would be sat at a table, given a drink or two, and asked to show the pictures to everyone. This disruption to pub life should have upset most licensees but not in this place! Yunnie usually went behind the bar, or waited on table, whilst the landlady and her customers sat in a corner, turning the pages of the album, enjoying the photographs. We certainly had some entertaining and informative evenings!

Each morning, after a good breakfast, I would leave Iain and Yunnie and savour the journey to Glenelg over Mam Ratagan; a zig-zag mountain pass constructed in 1815, rising from sea level to almost 1100 feet.

Sadly the road has been much changed since my first few trips. I mean no criticism of the high standard of work but it is my personal belief that such alterations have an adverse effect on the community they are supposed to benefit; like the motorway/dual carriage-way links to the English Lake District which allow millions of us, living in Lancashire and Cheshire, to be within a ninety minute drive of Windermere, Ambleside or Bowness, a town to be avoided on a summer Sunday afternoon. Glenelg, however, is certainly not like Bowness and traffic is still very light, but for how much longer? But if the money spent on Mam Ratagan, said to be around £800,000, brings local employment, then it *will* have been justified.

Some days my only hazard on the road would be the sheep, defiantly lying in the centre of the tarmac! And it was on such a morning, with the sun warming the dewy grass and the deep purple foxgloves waving from the lush green fern, that I descended the mountain for my second visit to Donna Dimambro.

The first batch of candles had just been completed when I arrived and an English couple were trying to decide on a purchase. I waited until they paid and departed the workshop. From a selection of large carrier bags, which kept the album safe from inclement weather, I produced the book and found a wax-free surface to rest it on.

'Would you like a coffee first?' enquired Donna.

'Yes please,' I said, never being one to refuse a hot drink anywhere, and with that she disappeared into the house, just a step away from the workshop, to emerge a few minutes later followed by a young man carrying three mugs of coffee.

'This is Eddie,' announced Donna. 'Can he look at the photographs too?'

And so began a fruitful and amazing day, the album pages being turned back and forth repeatedly as the information poured from my knowledgeable, willing guides.

'Those crofts are probably in Galtair,' suggested Eddie, as he perused the first group of Glenelg photographs. *(79)* 'We could go there after lunch and look for them.' I nodded eagerly. More pages scanned; more names suggested.

'Just look at this hammer thrower,' giggled Donna. 'Doesn't he look like Charlie!' *(87)* A reference to a local man who apparently had the same features as the person in the photograph. I checked that reference out much later but Charlie denied all family connections with the Victorian hammer thrower, although he certainly did resemble him a little!

'That's definitely Quarry,' said Donna, pointing to a particular photograph. 'And look, here's this house!' She exclaimed triumphantly. *(95-97)*

'Show me,' I said. 'I never spotted that!'

There was no reason why I should have done; it wasn't my village and this was only my third trip to the area. Donna patiently explained the lay-out of the houses in the area of Glenelg known as Quarry and their relationship to the later properties built after 1889 and, of course, the whole thing was simple. The clues were there but it needed local knowledge to work them out and Donna and Eddie had just that.

The atmosphere in the room was frantic and exciting and we had run out of cigarettes. I went to the car for another packet and Donna went off to make some more coffee. The hours had just slipped away.

When I returned with the cigarettes Eddie was standing near the door, a big grin on his face.

'I think I know where the Tinker Woman photo was taken,' he said. 'Look at the stone-work and gable end of the croft behind her.'

The full photographic image in the album shows the woman and girl standing in front of a thatched cottage, a large gable-ended house with distinctive stone work next door *(98)*.

At that moment Donna returned with the coffee.

'Donna, show Bob that picture of this house again,' said Eddie.

She handed a cup of coffee over, wiped her hands and turned the pages until she found the right photograph. Eddie stabbed at the image triumphantly.

'There, look at the house next door!' he said quietly. 'Now look at the Tinker Woman.' He stood back and the two of us leaned forward.

'Eddie, she's standing outside this house!' screamed Donna. I was stunned and not just from the piercing noise!

There we all were, in the very house that the Tinker Woman had actually called at in 1889. Because of the changes to the building over the years we had failed to recognize it immediately. My own instinctive reaction was to go outside, stand on the exact spot and stare towards the piece of road, yards away, where the camera and tripod rested on that summer day so long ago. I was that close to a little piece of history and I was enjoying the discovery!

Donna prepared the lunch, a tasty, healthy affair full of vegetables, fruit and cheese, and as the three of us sat there I learnt more about my table companion, Eddie Stiven, a champion for the cause of the 'Scots' language and a writer of at least ten radio and screen plays in that language. A particular stage success had been *'Tamlane'*, a play which had been well received by audience and critics alike during an Edinburgh Festival, but his pressing priority for the following year, 1987, was not the Festival in Edinburgh but the Gala in Glenelg, a week of festivities which would end with the annual Highland Games and a ceilidh, and Eddie was looking for something different to accompany the event.

Calum Stiven and his mother, Donna, on the exact spot where a century before stood the Tinker Woman, also with her young son, Solomon. See No. 98. (Photo: Cailean Maclean).

'Would you be interested in putting on a show of some of the photographs next year?' he asked.

An opportunity to show my find to the residents of Glenelg, and the summer visitors, was just what I wanted and I didn't hesitate.

'I'd be delighted! If you can find me the space, I'll find the time.'

The eventual plan was that the village hall be hired and used for a public exhibition of the pictures, and that it be open to all, free of charge, during the Gala Week in July. That night I rang Sandra and told her the news.

'I hope you know what you are letting yourself in for,' she said, ever cautious. 'Have you got enough information so far?'

'No, but I will have by next year,' I replied confidently, and she laughed.

I returned home at the end of that week, my head reeling with plans. Good note-taking is as essential to a police officer as to a journalist and I had learnt my trade with some of the best detectives in Lancashire, so I wasn't short of facts but my Gaelic spelling was terrible and every map I studied gave a different version anyway!

This was not going to be easy and in fact we made many more journeys to Kintail, Letterfearn and Glenelg, enjoying Yunnie's wonderful hospitality whilst we completed the arrangements for the Gala and refined the notes.

No one keeps a secret – well not for too long – in this part of the Highlands and Yunnie was persuasive in winning a one day preview of the photographs on her side of Mam Ratagan, Kintail.

As the tourist board representative for the district, she had made it her mission in life to see that all the thousands of people who drove through Kintail on their way to the Isle of Skye should stop and spend some money in the area, or at least slow down and enjoy the free view.

A Saturday event in Kintail Village Hall, she assured me, would stop a few coaches and, of course, 'hundreds of local people will turn up' she had added, decisively.

Heaven help them later on if they don't, I thought!

On that Saturday in July, 1987, at 10 a.m. the doors of the hall were opened to the public.

Fifty sepia toned enlargements, 20 x 16 inches, had been prepared for the display by a young, enthusiastic photographer friend of mine living near Chester, Michael Day. I had given him the painstaking task of rephotographing all the original pictures so that if anything should ever happen to the album then at least there would be an archive record of the 1889 images. This was becoming very important as more people were asking to see the album and the risk of damage was increasing.

Mike worked long and hard to get the exposure times correct and then select the right grade of photographic paper for the print itself. The sepia toning effect could be a very hit and miss affair and it was important that it should match, as close as possible, the original Victorian colour. What he achieved was to my personal satisfaction and he continues to do excellent work with the images to this day.

That first public showing of the photographs prepared us for the future. Yunnie had been right, of course! The response was totally overwhelming and hundreds of people did come through the doors; in fact we had to beg people to leave at 7 p.m., one hour after the official closing time. Again It was to lead to us meeting some wonderful people with facts and figures to impart.

BBC *Radio nan Gaidheal* produced a piece on the exhibition and interviewed, in Gaelic, a local man, Eddie MacRae, who had a great knowledge of the area and could identify most of the anonymous fields, walls and crofts in the photographs of Letterfearn and Kintail. Eddie did much to encourage local interest in the collection and I was saddened when I learnt of his untimely death in autumn 1990.

The following day, Sunday, the exhibits were loaded into the car and transported across the mountain. The photographs had been mounted on to half inch chipboard to keep them rigid and durable. It was a mistake that I would not make again for they were bulky and very heavy!

The Glenelg show was to last for six days from the Monday, opening at 10 a.m. and closing at 5.00 p.m., with free admission and coffee available most of the day. Donna had put up posters around the village and everyone was aware that *'the Englishman with the old photos'* was to be at the hall all week.

It became impossible to count the number of people who came through the doors.

Some, mostly visitors, came once only and spent ten minutes or so looking at the images.

Others came from far away, having heard the radio interview or received a report from a friend. Local people came frequently, especially the older male inhabitants of the village who usually arrived in groups of three or four each morning of the exhibition, staying for thirty minutes at a time.

Chatting in the Gaelic they kept us out of the conversation but it was not a discourtesy, it was after all their native language and they were going to let us in on the secrets on the last day when the group spokesman, John Angus MacRae, produced a list of the sites and names of some of the people in the pictures, especially those competing in the Highland Games.

On the Wednesday the exhibition was visited by, amongst others, a lady and her mother. For almost an hour they walked around the hall, discussing and looking closely at all of the photographs. At the end of their stay the lady came up to me.

'Do you have any more pictures like these?' she asked politely.

'Well, yes I do, but I could only bring these with me,' I ventured. 'There just wasn't space for any more.'

'Are the originals in an album?'

'Yes they are. In fact there are about 250 from all over Scotland in the collection.' I replied.

'Do you think I could see the album?'

'Unfortunately the album is a bit fragile,' I said apologetically. 'And the risk of damage is too great especially when turning the pages.'

'I promise I will be very careful,' she said with some persistence.

'But everyone says that to me!' I insisted, with as much good humour as possible.

There was a pause, and then the lady extended her arm and held out a business card. I took it, blushed, apologised and offered to get the album from the back of the car. I may be the present guardian of the collection but who could refuse Dr. Ann Matheson, MA, MLitt, PhD, Keeper, Department of Printed Books at the National Library of Scotland in Edinburgh, the right to examine my find? I have met Ann many times since that day and still enjoy telling this story whenever there is an audience!

Another who came to see the exhibition was a great character, Ross Noble, the kilted, much travelled curator of the Highland Folk Museum at Kingussie. Ross has given a lot of his precious time to assist in researching the photographs and in 1988 he hosted the collection as his Summer Exhibition. This museum is a fun place and it cannot be recommended too highly. The children will love it and if you are ever on the A9, heading to or away from Inverness, you must come off at Kingussie and pay a visit; you will not regret it.

At the end of that week in Glenelg, in August, 1987, many more people were familiar with the photos of the still anonymous photographer. Much had been gathered from those living locally as to the places shown in the photographs and of course there had been a great deal of discussion and speculation as to who the individuals might have been.

Fine weather had also enabled me to walk to some of the nearby sites in the photographs and recheck the locations, and I spent many an hour wandering through Galtair, following the advice of the much travelled author, Alasdair Alpin MacGregor, who wrote in *'Somewhere in Scotland'* (Robert Hale Ltd., 1935):

'If ever you go to Glenelg, you should linger along the ancient drove-road to Kylerhea at the witching hour, when darkness has silenced the bustling world of men, and the firmament is hung with stars.'

It was on that very drove-road in Galtair that the tinkers set up their camp in 1889, and at the *'witching hour'* on a cool summer evening in 1989 I walked to the spot. *(76)*

A caravan was parked there but the *'bustling world of men'* had not been silenced that particular night. A radio was being played too loudly, but perhaps it had been the wail of the bagpipes a century earlier!

But the question most asked during my week in Glenelg was: *'Who took the pictures?'*

This of course was the dominant question underlying the quest and to resolve this by establishing the identity of our enigmatic photographer would be the equivalent of establishing the authorship of an anonymous manuscript, or the painter of an unsigned masterpiece.

Here, however, was the problem, for the only real clue contained in the album was the picture of a lady at a picnic in Aultbea, Ross-shire *(45)*, who also appeared on the steps of a mansion in Combe Hay, near Bath. *(122)*

Not until the end of 1988, three months after the Kingussie exhibition (and the same old question regarding the identity of the photographer), did we decide to journey down the M6 and M5 motorways to Bath in pursuit of this slender thread; the first fingerprint which might lead to a name!

The late Victorian explorer in fair weather...

CHAPTER THREE

The Photographer Revealed!

On 25 November, 1988, we drove down to Bath for a four day Christmas shopping trip.

Well that was Sandra's excuse! I had already decided to approach the staff at the Royal Photographic Society (RPS) in Bath and seek their professional help with the album, so there was a second excuse.

But both only thinly veiled an urge to find the house in Combe Hay as perhaps holding some clue to the identity of the photographer and the two people shown standing on the steps of that house in 1889.

The following day I kept my appointment with the RPS and the album was examined avidly by members of staff, but despite this attention they were unable to suggest a possible name for the photographer. We had, perhaps, hoped for a miracle. My judgment was that the unknown cameraman was good, that his style would be instantly recognized by the experts, and his name would be handed to me on a glass plate. That was not the case!

The shopping in Bath took longer than anticipated but what do men know about buying early Christmas presents?

It was day three before we found Combe Hay, a delightful English village that can have changed little since the photographs were taken in the 1880s. A narrow, tree-lined, road wanders through this place of considerable peace and charm, and we stopped outside the ancient church. I parked and got out of the car clutching copies of all the Combe Hay pictures in the album. Sandra followed me.

A young man in his early thirties was standing nearby and we went up to him.

'Excuse me,' I said. 'Do you have any idea where this building is?' and I handed him the photograph of the two fashionably dressed people standing on some steps outside a house.

'Oh yes, just follow me,' he replied after a few seconds. We walked a few yards, up a private drive at the side of the village church, and stopped in front of a large mansion.

'There they are!' exclaimed Sandra, pointing towards a flight of steps leading to a door, and indeed they were; virtually unaltered since 1889. *(122)*

'This is a very old picture,' said the young man. 'Who took it?'

'If only we knew!' sighed Sandra, whose mind was probably more on the shops of Bath than these steps in Combe Hay.

'Are the owners at home?' I asked of the young man but he shook his head.

'No, they're away in the Far East just now.' That was a pity.

I always like to show to present day owners, photographs of their property taken in times past and the current residents of this particular property might have been able to answer some of my questions about the occupier in the Victorian period.

Here, at this very house, a middle aged lady had been photographed in 1889. One other picture in the album showed her at a picnic in Aultbea, Scotland, so she had to have known our anonymous photographer. But was this her English home or did it belong to the unseen man behind the camera?

'Do you happen to know who lived here in the last century?' I asked hopefully.

'Sorry. I'm afraid not.'

We thanked him and walked back to the car. I had an idea.

'We're going back to Bath,' I announced, 'and you can carry on with your shopping whilst I go to the reference library. We'll meet up after an hour.' Sandra beamed.

At the library I found the 1889 *'Kelly's Directory'*, a useful book which lists towns and villages within a specific county and gives details of the post offices, posting times, market days, the local gentry and such-like. Under the entry for Combe Hay was the following: *'Dr. John Cass Smart is lord of the manor and principal landowner and resides at the Manor House Combe Hay'*.

So now I had the name of the occupier at the time the photograph had been taken, but it still left me wanting some answers to questions I could not ask of any one person in particular.

Had this *Dr. John Cass Smart* taken the photographs in Scotland and Combe Hay in 1889 or were we on the wrong track altogether? He certainly knew the lady who was standing on the steps of his house but who was she? His wife, his sister or mother perhaps? The possibilities were endless and I could see no way to resolve that part of our quest with any ease.

I went back to our prearranged meeting place and waited for Sandra.

'Well what did you find out?' were her first words when she arrived. I told her.

'I've just walked past the local newspaper office, why don't you try there?'

Thank you Dr. Watson, I thought, why didn't I think of that one!

At the front desk of the newspaper office I asked the receptionist if I could speak to a reporter, and after a minute or so a young lady came down the stairs from the news-room.

I handed her a copy of the Combe Hay Manor House photograph and told her of my quest, emphasising the importance of the image. I could see she was not impressed one bit.

'I will offer a cash reward to the first reader of your paper who can name the photographer!' I announced grandly.

'How much of a reward?' she asked. Was that a yawn she was trying to hide behind her hand?

'Fifty pounds!' I heard myself saying. Sandra groaned.

'Right, you're on. I'll put it in the paper next week,' said the girl with a smirk on her face, and I thought I heard a sob alongside me as we walked towards the door.

'You must be mad!' exclaimed Sandra on the pavement outside. 'What if someone comes up with any old name? How are you going to prove it?'

'Deduction,' I replied. 'Deduction! Anyway it has to be worth fifty pounds of anyone's money to have the name of the photographer,' I argued, but Sandra was half way down the street and out of ear-shot and I was getting strange looks from the passing shoppers.

The following day we returned to Combe Hay for a second look at the village as the first trip had been so brief. We parked in the same spot outside the church and went inside. I had an idea that, as principal landowner in 1889, Dr. John Smart would have been an important benefactor and may have had a memorial tablet erected after his death. It was worth a try anyway.

And sure enough it was there, on the wall of the church, just yards from his old home. It contained details of his wife and children as an extra bonus.

John Cass Smart MD of Combe Hay Manor,
formerly of Scarboro and Tunbridge Wells.
Born 10.12.1815., died 14.7.1894.,
and his wife:
Mabel Ellerby, born 6.7.1815., died 29.10.1908.

And their children:
Francis Gray Smart MB, of Tunbridge Wells.
Born 25.1.1844., died 7.4.1913.

George Edward, of Combe Hay Manor.
Born 5.11.1849., died 14.1.1939.

Margaret, of Combe Hay Manor.
Born 20.3.1853., died 5.10.1920.

The trip had been worthwhile and we returned home satisfied with our few days in Bath.

A few weeks went by and we were still waiting for a response to the Combe Hay picture in the Bath newspaper. I realised that it would be a long shot but I had hoped that the present owners of the house might have returned home for Christmas and had been made aware of the photograph. And whilst the trip to Bath had been very successful and we had the family name of Smart to work with, I had no proof that Dr. John Cass Smart was our elusive photographer. But there was still much work to do on the Scottish photographs and I was in the middle of some research, on the evening of 21st December, 1988, when the telephone rang.

'Hello, is that Mr. Charnley?' asked a female caller.

'Yes it is.'

'Mr. Charnley, I live in Combe Hay and I have seen that photograph of the Manor House you sent to the local paper.'

'Oh good,' I replied. 'I wasn't sure if they had printed it yet.'

'Well it was a few weeks ago now but I have only just got hold of your telephone number from the paper and I thought I would ring you with the news.'

Keep calm, I told myself.

'What news is that?' I asked anxiously.

'I know who took your photograph!' she said laughing.

My caller, Freda Shellard, then went on to tell me who she was, where she lived in the village (we had parked opposite her house during our visit) and how her father had been head gardener to Mr. George Edward Smart, at the Manor House, in the Thirties.

She recounted how Mr. George, the younger son of Dr. John Cass Smart, was considered an eccentric recluse; but her father had got on well with him and Mr. George would show him family photographs which he said had been taken by his brother *Francis Gray Smart*, a well-known photographer living in Tunbridge Wells.

Before ringing me, explained Freda, she had been in touch with a close friend, June Cooling, who lived near-by in the village of Dunkerton, and having conferred together they had agreed that Francis Smart *must* be the man I was looking for.

This would be a wonderful Christmas present if I could prove it and I thanked Freda, promising to pay the reward as soon as I had followed up the story. She wished me luck and a Happy Christmas and rang off!

Sandra grinned when I told her the news.

'Looks like you've lost your money!' she said. 'But the news is good.'

Francis Gray Smart! Was this the name of the man we were looking for? It appeared to be very promising!

Christmas came and went; the winter set in and we hibernated.

I was keen to be on the trail of Francis Smart but a couple of trips to Scotland had been planned before Easter and Tunbridge Wells was too far in the wrong direction. It was now 1989 and the photographs would be one hundred years old in the summer. I was determined to end our quest for the photographer in the centenary year.

Eventually, some three months after the news from Combe Hay, I managed to find a couple of spare days and drove down to Tunbridge Wells, arriving just before 10 a.m. on a warm March morning. Having found a good parking spot I went to the Public Library, the first calling-place for any research of this nature. In fact I was hoping to find an obituary notice for Francis Gray Smart in the newspaper for the second week of April, 1913, the week after his death according to the memorial tablet in Combe Hay church.

I explained to the librarian, Jean Mauldon, what I was looking for and she kindly set up the microfilm of the 1913 edition of the *'Kent and Sussex Courier'* on the machine. I turned to the obituary columns for April. Nothing. Wrong week maybe. Go back one. Nothing. Well perhaps the family had not informed the paper or, worse still, he had died in another town. All this way for nothing! I groaned inwardly and very audibly.

'Everything all right?' enquired Miss Mauldon over my right shoulder, as I continued to turn the handle of the machine, aimlessly now, scanning the pages with no great interest.

'Yes, great thanks!' I exclaimed, as the headline, five inches wide, over a photograph of a venerable, white-bearded gentleman, leapt from the page: *'DEATH OF MR. F. G. SMART. It is with deep regret that we record the death of Mr. Francis Gray Smart....'*

I sat back in the chair, staring at the mass of words in front of me. This was some obituary, 66 column inches long, monopolizing five columns, and I had been looking for a brief paragraph! Was this, then, our enigmatic and elusive traveller; the artist behind the photographic images? The man who had started both of us on a twentieth century adventure of discovery?

I read on:

'It is with deep regret that we record the death of Mr. Francis Gray Smart, M.A., J.P., of Bredbury and Oakhurst, Tunbridge Wells.

The deceased gentleman had for some time past been seriously ill, and passed away on Monday morning last at one o'clock, in the 70th year of his age, he having celebrated his 69th birthday in January last. Mr. Smart had never really recovered from an accident two years ago in London, when he was knocked down by a motor car, and although it was then hoped that he had escaped serious injury, he had been in failing health ever since.

A tragic circumstance of his illness was that his devoted wife had a fortnight ago to unexpectedly undergo an operation, from which she did not recover, and the last time Mr. Smart saw his wife was when she visited his sickroom before the operation. Mr. Smart was too weak to be moved afterwards, and did not see his wife again, and it was obvious that he was gradually sinking, notwithstanding the devoted attendance of Dr. Neild, his nurse (Mr. Russell), and his butler (Mr. Smith). Those who were present at Bredbury were Mr. T.G. Duncanson (nephew of Mrs. Smart), Miss Smart (sister) and Miss Mary Smart (cousin).

The bulletins, which were daily posted at Bredbury, were watched with painful interest, and the news of the end was received with deep regret by a very wide circle.

It may be said of Mr. and Mrs. Smart that, devoted as they were in life, they were in death not divided. Theirs was indeed a life of devotion, not only to each other, but to mutual good works. In their death the poor of the town have lost two of their greatest benefactors. When Mr. and Mrs. Smart celebrated their silver wedding two years ago, the happy event was marked by munificent gifts to various charities, and notably a subscription in four figures to the Endowment Fund of the Homoeopathic Hospital. Mrs. Smart was always a generous supporter of charities, particularly the General Hospital, and in this work of benevolence Mr. Smart delighted to co-operate. Their names will long be remembered in Tunbridge Wells with honour and gratitude for many kindly and generous deeds.

The late Mr. Smart, who was a son of the late Dr. Smart, had lived 40 years in Tunbridge Wells, and took a keen interest in the welfare of the town, although he had never taken any part in its local administration beyond acting as a Justice of the Peace when placed on the Commission of the Peace for Kent.

In other respects, however, Mr. Smart rendered valuable public service, specially in connection with the Homoeopathic Hospital, of which he was the President of the Council, and took an active part in the securing of the new Hospital premises and their adequate equipment, as well as the creation of an endowment fund. The Hospital may be said to owe its existence in its present form to the continued generosity of Mr. and Mrs. Smart. The General Hospital and the Ear and Eye Hospital, as well as the Nursing Association, were literally supported by Mr. and Mrs. Smart, while Holy Trinity Church and parish had in them great benefactors. The church organ was the gift of Mrs. Smart, while the restoration of the church some years ago was largely facilitated by their generosity.

It is an interesting fact that Mr. and Mrs. Smart, in order that their benefactions should not clash, were accustomed to each take an individual interest in particular objects, and there were, we believe, several hundred subscriptions given by them annually to various societies and charitable objects, which were classified in admirable business order.

Mr. F. G. Smart, M.A., J.P.

One of their most notable benefactions outside Tunbridge Wells was the gift of two lifeboats to the National Lifeboat Institution, one being stationed at Barmouth and the other at New Quay, Cardiganshire. These were named by the Christian names of their donors, Frank and Marion.'

At this point the reporter went on to list the educational and scientific interests of Mr. Smart, resuming:

'Another scientific pursuit of Mr. Smart's was Botany. The Gardens of Bredbury were a wonder and a delight, while the carefully planned rock gardens, with their many rare specimens, were famous in horticultural circles. Masses of flowers were loved by Mr. and Mrs. Smart and those privileged to attend their garden parties in the summer months will not easily forget the beautiful effects of colour in the Bredbury Gardens.'

But it was the next paragraph that sent shivers up and down my spine as I read:

'Photography was another art in which Mr. Smart was a distinguished amateur. He was President of the Tunbridge Wells Photographic Association, and for many years took an active interest in its success. The achievements in picture photography by Mr. Smart

were always a notable feature of the exhibition of the Association locally, as well as at the great Photographic Exhibition in London, where Mr. Smart's architectural and other studies were much admired for their high artistic merit and technique. Those privileged to witness the exhibition by lantern projection of Mr. Smart's work in his studio will recall the surprising amount of photographic work Mr. Smart found time to do, while the annual visit to Bredbury while Mr. Smart's health permitted was always a red letter day with the members of the Tunbridge Wells Photographic Association.'

I had found the proof at last and there could be no doubt about it. Francis Gray Smart was our photographer, anonymous no longer. But how busy he had been. I had to know more!

'When the Congress of Homoeopathic Doctors was held some years ago, Mr. and Mrs. Smart gave a reception at Bredbury, and there was a notable gathering of celebrities in the homoeopathic world.

As a collector Mr. Smart showed great taste and judgment. A lover of books, his library may with one great exception be considered the first in the neighbourhood of any private collection. Works of antiquarian and topographical interest, art and colour books in the editions de luxe, and a botanical library, were the principal directions in which Mr. Smart was a collector, and his library had extended to thousands of volumes. He was President of the local Dudley Institute and considerably augmented its library. As a collector of ivories, Mr. Smart had brought together a collection of rare interest and of

Members of the Tunbridge Wells Amateur Photographic Assocation, wives, husbands and friends, at the home of their President, Francis Smart, in 1908. The photograph is said to have been taken by Joseph Chamberlain, founder member and, at various times, Hon. Secretary or Treasurer of the Association. He was also private secretary to Francis Smart who is seated on the front row in this picture. Even with a time delay on the camera there is cause for doubt as to the attribution of the photographer; Joseph Chamberlain is the bearded gentleman on the back row, third from the right. (Photo courtesy Tunbridge Wells Library Collection)

exquisite workmanship, while his collection of medals was one of great historical value.'

At this point the reporter revealed the deceased gentleman's interest in politics and his London clubs, concluding: *'...it may be recalled that Mr. Smart had a long list of honorific distinctions Having graduated M.A. (Caius College, Cambridge) and M.B., he was also F.L.S., F.R.Met.S., F.R.G.S., F.A.S., and F.R.B.S. He was also a J.P. for Kent and the Patron of one Living, viz., Combe Hay, near Bath.*

But we have said enough to indicate what were Mr. Smart's many sided activities and cultured breadth of interests. In his death a great loss has been sustained, and one which all classes in the town will deplore. Although his failing health of the last two years precluded his appearance in public meetings, and he resigned one or two offices which he held, he maintained till almost the last his keen interest in his various experimental work, and in this respect he was spared a good deal of fatigue which might have made the continuance of the work impossible in his state of health, by the devoted co-operation of his secretary, Mr. Joseph Chamberlain, whose services were invaluable. Thus until increasing physical weakness overpowered Mr. Smart's indomitable energy, it may be said that he lived a full life of crowded hours of scientific usefulness, of artistic interest, and last, but not least, of far-reaching benevolence. These interests were shared by his beloved wife, and their deaths, within a few days of each other, when, humanly speaking, it appeared that Mrs. Smart would outlive her husband, is a double loss which will be grievously felt, not only by their wide circle of friends, but by the numerous recipients of their bounty. The town generally will unite in mourning the loss of two of its most esteemed as well as oldest residents'.

Here the paper reports the events surrounding the funeral, the music played, the names of the mourners and those who sent wreathes. But the list of *'immediate mourners'* revealed just a little of his life style:

'Miss Smart (sister), Misses Mary and Susie Smart (cousins), Mr. and Mrs. Duncanson, Mr. and Mrs. Ford Duncanson, the Misses Duncanson (2), Dr. and Mrs. Thomas, Miss Buckle, Mr. Hall, Dr. Neild, the Master of Gonville and Caius College, Cambridge, Colonel Sydney (also representing the College), Mr. Joseph Chamberlain (Mr. Smart's secretary), Mr. Russell (nurse), Mr. Owen Smith (butler), Mrs. Goldsmith (housekeeper), Miss Waterman (maid), Mr. Richardson (head gardener), and 18 other servants.'

Obviously a very wealthy, middle class, Victorian gentleman with a staff numbering twenty two, but how pleasing to see they were treated as part of the family, and immediate mourners, rather than being left outside the church as 'just the servants'.

The final paragraph of the obituary was a report of the tribute paid to both Mr. and Mrs. Smart by the vicar of Holy Trinity Church, Tunbridge Wells, at the annual vestry meeting, great stress being placed upon their tremendous charity. The whole obituary is a moving account of a couple devoted to their causes in life and I was to discover more of their great generosity at a later date.

I stood up from the machine and stretched my arms and legs. I am not sure how Miss Mauldon interpreted the movements but she came across the room from behind her desk.

'How have you got on?' She asked, concern in her voice. 'Did you find what you wanted?'

I told her, very briefly, of my quest. Librarians hear enough personal family details from researchers tracing ancestors and I didn't want to bore her as she had been most helpful!

'If Mr. Smart was the President of the Photographic Society you might like to see a few early documents we have in the files.'

It was not a question but a statement of fact she was making, and within a minute she returned with a thin folder.

'Not very much but it may help,' she said, handing it over.

Inside I found a booklet about the Tunbridge Wells Amateur Photographic Association and on page ten the four line entry: *'In 1913 the Association suffered a sad loss in the death of Francis Smart who had been President since the founding of the Association in 1887 and who had been generous in his hospitality and financial support.'* That brief sentence was of some significance, for it proved Mr. Smart had an interest in photography prior to 1889, the year of the 'Scotch Tour' photographs.

Also in the folder, wrapped in brown paper, was a small book; a copy of the *'Catalogue of the 6th Annual Exhibition of the Tunbridge Wells Amateur Photographic Association'*.

Held in the Royal Sussex Assembly Rooms, Tunbridge Wells, on two days in November, 1892, it had been opened by the President himself, Francis Gray Smart, and he was exhibiting some of his own photographs.

In various Classes he submitted pictures. Class X 'Figure Studies' included *'Fisherman mending his Net'* which might have been the photograph taken in Nairn showing a fisherman with his net, closely watched by a group of children *(38)*.

But it was in Class VIII 'Prints from Negatives taken with a Hand Camera' that there appeared the following entry for the President: *'Oban, Early Morning' (111), 'Tossing the Caber' (89)* and *'Sack Race'. (93)* All these photographs appear in the 1889 album, the last two having been taken during the Glenelg Games in the August of that year. This was, indeed, the final irrefutable evidence that Francis Gray Smart was our remarkable photographer.

That just left me with two pieces of unfinished business to deal with when I returned home. The reward to Freda Shellard in Combe Hay, who put me on the final leg of the search, and a letter to the present secretary of the Tunbridge Wells Photographic Association.

Freda shared the reward with June Cooling and the total was donated to charities.

The secretary of the Photographic Association replied to my letter concerning the whereabouts of Francis Smart's camera equipment and photograph collection by saying that they had no knowledge of anything that had belonged to their first President.

We found out for ourselves, some eighteen months later, what happened to these items after the death of Francis Smart, but more of that later.

And so the search was over.

We had gone back a century in time to find a man from a very different world to ours. But great advances in science and technology were already happening during the later years of Francis Smart's life; electricity, motor driven vehicles, men flying, radio telegraphy and so on.

But he was also to know the tragedy of the Boer War, the death of Queen Victoria and her son Edward, and the loss of the Titanic. At least he was spared the massive hurt of the World War that was to come.

His generosity was apparently limitless and there can be little doubt that his staff were entirely devoted to both him and his wife Marion. The impact on the household, all twenty two of them, when they lost both Mistress and Master within eight days must have been crushing.

That this small part of his photographic legacy survived is testimony to the quality of his art and resurrecting the personality behind its creation further illuminates the work itself. No large hunting-lodges with kilted noblemen in rigid poses cover the pages of his album. Neither are to be found here memorabilia of sporting parties amidst a sea of gun-dogs.

That was not the world of a Southern English Victorian philanthropist and Justice of the Peace, passionately devoted to a study of the sciences, the collection of rare books, ivories, coins and medals. His motivation was a curiosity about people and the landscapes which shaped their lives, be it on a railway platform in Edinburgh or from the ferry landing-stage at Glenelg.

The album is a story largely without words, a complex portrayal of societies within society. And if his images possess compelling vigour, it is precisely because he could view humanity with the eye of an artist and at the same time fix that image with the skills of a scientist.

. . . and foul!

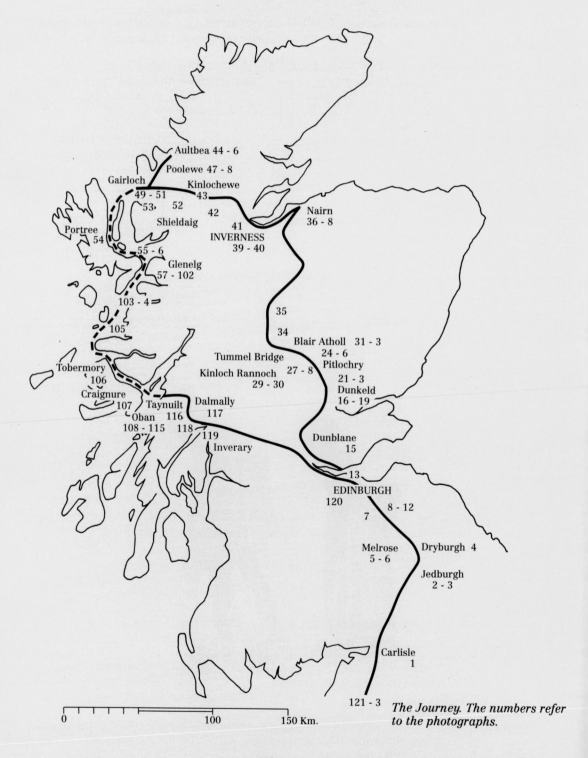

Aultbea 44 - 6
Poolewe 47 - 8
Gairloch   Kinlochewe
49 - 51   43
53·   52   42   Nairn
Shieldaig   41   36 - 8
INVERNESS
Portree   39 - 40
54
55 - 6
Glenelg
57 - 102

103 - 4

105   35

34
Blair Atholl 31 - 3
Tummel Bridge   24 - 6
Kinloch Rannoch   27 - 8   Pitlochry
Tobermory   29 - 30   21 - 3
106   Dunkeld
Craignure   16 - 19
107   Taynuilt   Dalmally
Oban   116   117
108 - 115   118
119   Dunblane
Inverary   15

13
EDINBURGH
120
7   8 - 12

Melrose   Dryburgh 4
5 - 6
Jedburgh
2 - 3

Carlisle
1

0   100   150 Km.

121 - 3   *The Journey. The numbers refer*
to the photographs.

CHAPTER FOUR

In Francis Smart's Footsteps

During most of the summer months of 1988, especially whilst the photographs were on show at the Highland Folk Museum in Kingussie, we called at some of the places visited by Francis Smart whilst travelling between Edinburgh, Inverness and Gairloch. At this time he had not been identified and was still just our 'anonymous' cameraman.

A spot on BBC Radio Scotland's *'Macgregor's Gathering'*, a popular morning programme, eased progress through Dunkeld, Pitlochry, Blair Atholl and Nairn, and considerable help was received with precise locations of the photographs.

In particular a great debt is owing to Robert Robertson of Pitlochry for all his help in identifying most of sites around Perthshire. He typified the generous attitude of all those whose enthusiasm has been stimulated by seeing the album.

It was of course always a delight to stand on an 'exact spot' and compare the nineteenth-century image with what lay before us.

Many of the sites had changed little, as at the Loch Tummel Inn, where the same kind attention and food was received that must have been given to the Smarts when they stopped there. *(27)*

Tummel Bridge itself was just a little different. A large complex, the Tummel Valley Holiday Park, covers the area by the river bank that the Smarts must have strolled along when they took a photograph of the bridge. *(28)* Further on, at Kinloch Rannoch, where Francis noticed a group of children playing on the grass whilst their mothers did the washing, the site today stands alongside a garage and the debris of the motoring age litters the spot. Not a safe place for small children now! *(29)*

CALEDONIAN RAILWAY.

TOURS IN SCOTLAND.

The CALEDONIAN RAILWAY COMPANY have arranged a system of TOURS—about seventy in number—by rail, steamer, and coach, comprehending almost every place of interest either for scenery or historical associations throughout Scotland, including—

EDINBURGH, GLASGOW, ABERDEEN, DUNDEE, INVERNESS, GREENOCK, PAISLEY, DUMFRIES, PEEBLES, STIRLING, PERTH, CRIEFF, DUNKELD, OBAN, INVERARAY,
The Trosachs, Loch-Katrine, Loch-Lomond, Loch-Earn, Loch-Tay, Loch-Awe, Caledonian Canal, Glencoe, Iona, Staffa, Skye, Balmoral, Braemar, Arran, Bute, The Firth of Clyde, The Falls of Clyde, &c., &c.

☞ TOURISTS are recommended to procure a copy of the Caledonian Railway Company's "Tourist Guide," which can be had at any of the company's stations, and also at the chief stations on the London and North-Western Railway, and which contains descriptive notices of the districts embraced in the tours, maps, plans, bird's-eye view, &c.

Tickets for these tours are issued at the company's booking offices at all the large stations.

The Tourist Season generally extends from June to September inclusive.

The Caledonian Company also issue Tourist Tickets to the Lake District of England, the Isle of Man, Connemara, the Lakes of Killarney, &c.

A Caledonian Railway advertisment from the 1880's.

Superficially little has changed in Dunkeld since the 1880s.

Visitors can still see most of the buildings that Francis photographed during the tour although they may be surprised to see the church, that he might have entered, selling the furniture that was new a century ago. Antiques now fill this former place of worship. *(16)*

Pitlochry, however, *has* altered over the years and we found it difficult to get our bearings. Gone was the Reading Room that graced the road in the 1880's, gone the turreted building which many remember as Prince Charlie's House. *(22)* An environmentally friendly petrol station stands in their place and photography at this place in the summer months would be a danger to life. The photographer's life!

From all these towns and villages the journey continued north towards Nairn and Inverness. Surprisingly few photographs of Inverness appear in the album, fewer in fact than Nairn.

Francis visited and photographed the Episcopal Cathedral *(40)*, and the Harbour *(39)* but, for whatever reason, did not take any pictures of the people or streets of the City. Perhaps it was raining too much.

Of his Nairn photos two are little gems *(37 & 38)* and, with some twelve or more other images from the Scotch Tour, they have now been issued as postcards by a leading company based in Fort William. Although the idea of reproducing the photographs on

Pitlochry in 1990; taken from the same spot as photo 22 in 1889. Under the lamp-post, on the right, is a six-chimney stack on the roof of the Bank of Scotland. This is the only building that Francis Smart would recognise from his own 1889 photograph. So much has changed in this small town in one hundred years.

postcard was undertaken as a commercial enterprise, it was prompted by a request from a Curriculum Development Officer with an Education Department, for copies of the photographs to be used in the classroom.

The Smarts would surely have approved their use.

From Inverness, though, their journey became more of an adventure, and the photographs reflect the nature and rugged grandeur of the area they were passing through.

At Glen Docherty Francis was able to photograph the great valley with Loch Maree in the distance *(42)*, a virtual impossibility today thanks to the trees that cover this district; whilst alongside the loch he paused to record the scene, his picture showing the great splendour and dominance of Ben Slioch, 3200 feet high. *(43)*

Francis and Marion must surely have been aware that they were travelling the route taken by Her Majesty Queen Victoria in 1877, when she visited the area and spent six nights in the Loch Maree Hotel. But did Francis Smart know that in 1863 George Washington Wilson, Scottish Photographer Royal, travelled the exact route that he and his wife Marion were taking? From Inverness Wilson, with his camera, called at the Falls of Rojie, Achnasheen, Kinlochewe, Loch Maree and Gairloch, photographing as much as he could in spite of the bad weather he encountered.

A full account of this trip, and of the life of pioneer photographer *George Washington* Wilson (1823-1893), appears in an excellent book of the same title by Roger Taylor, published by Aberdeen University Press in 1981.

As a generation of people, the Victorian British travelled further afield than anyone

PITLOCHRIE.
FISHER'S HOTEL.
FIRST-CLASS FAMILY HOTEL
AND
POSTING ESTABLISHMENT.

PARTIES wishing to see the magnificent Scenery in this part of the Scottish Highlands will find this Hotel (to which large additions have been made) most convenient, for in One Drive they can visit the
Falls of Tummel, the Queen's View of Loch Tummel;
The Far-Famed Pass of Killiecrankie;
Glen Tilt; The Falls of Bruar, &c.
Pitlochrie is on the direct route to Balmoral Castle, by Spittal of Glenshee and Braemar; and to Taymouth Castle and Kinloch-Rannoch, by Tummel Bridge.
Salmon and Trout Fishing on the Rivers Tummel and Garry, and on the Lochs in the neighbourhood.
EXCURSION COACHES
leave the Hotel daily during the summer season for Pass of Killiecrankie, Falls of Bruar, Queen's View on Loch Tummel, Kinloch-Rannoch, Glen Tilt, &c. Seats secured at the Hotel. Fares moderate.
Job and Post Horses and Carriages of every kind,
By the Day, Week, or Month.
ORDERS BY TELEGRAPH FOR ROOMS, CARRIAGES, OR COACH SEATS, PUNCTUALLY ATTENDED TO.

An advertisement from the mid-1880s for Fisher's Hotel, Pitlochry. It was still common for one or two of the hotels to cling to the old form of spelling 'Pitlochrie', but by the end of the decade the new version was accepted by all. It is possible that the Smarts used the Fisher's as their base in the district, as many still do today.

previously and their wealth came with an expertise in the travel industry, whether for pleasure or commerce. The motor car was just about to be born in 1889, in fact a steam powered tricycle was being demonstrated at the Paris Exhibition at this very time. Within months it became a four wheeled vehicle, fitted with a Daimler engine of one horsepower running on petrol. It carried the same badge as my own car does today; Peugeot. How ironic that it was to be a motor car that shortened the life of Francis Smart.

However, in 1889, they still had to rely on the horse-drawn coach and rail network for this part of their tour, and whilst the journey from Tunbridge Wells to Edinburgh, and then to Inverness, would present no problem, the rail line in some areas of the Scottish Highlands was still incomplete.

The 1889 *'Baddeley's Guide to Scotland'* examined the rail system at this time and reported that:

'The revolution that has taken place in railway travelling affords sufficient proof of the will of the public to travel if they can only find the way. Fairly well to do people whose grandfathers made, say, three 'grand tours' in a lifetime, nowadays arrange for an excursion every year, and the 'go where you please in comfort at a penny a mile' principle has incalculably extended the area of their wanderings. Under the old system they would either only go once, where now they go three times, or they would not go at all. If the tourist tickets of the visitors were examined any day at a first class hotel in Oban, a very large proportion of them would be found to be third class.'

At Achnasheen the couple would have found that this particular rail line ran out and the rest of the journey to Gairloch, just over twenty eight miles away, was by horse-drawn coach, a laborious trip of *five* hours in 1889.

What an uncomfortable time that must have been, and I remembered that far off journey when, in 1989, I sat with Harry Slater, a happy, contented Yorkshireman, in his Newtonmore restaurant discussing the old photographs over a cup of coffee. Outside the window a sleek, air conditioned coach, with tea making facilities and a toilet, pulled up and a few passengers boarded. It powered away, bound for the A9 and Inverness. It was called *'Stage Coach'* and represented a century of progress on our roads!

Thanks to a photograph in the album captioned *'from our window' (49)*, we know that our travellers, at the end of their five hour journey, stayed at the luxury Gairloch Hotel with its *'..numerous Public Rooms, Suites of Apartments and 150 Beds..'* as a contemporary guide book described it. They could relax at last and look forward to the various excursions that they were to undertake.

From Gairloch the couple visited Aultbea where they were fortunate in finding a group of children on the shore gathering whelks at low water. With cumbersome camera and plates ever ready, the Smarts picked their way across the wet and weed strewn rocks to record the scene and one more fine, beautifully composed, image was recorded on the glass negative.

The site of this photograph is very close to the Aultbea Hotel where Sandra and I have spent a few pleasant hours in the footsteps of Francis and Marion, enjoying the food and numerous cups of coffee, chatting with the much-travelled proprietor, Peter Nieto, and gazing out to those rocks.

It is possible to speculate with some accuracy about the nature of Francis Smart's camera equipment on this tour, thanks to information available in the photographic journals of the period and our knowledge that the album contains pictures of two sizes.

His principal image taker was a field camera, probably made in brass-bound mahogany with swing back and focusing screen. With it he would carry an array of lenses, some double dark slides, a bulky tripod and the ubiquitous black cloth. Such an amount of equipment required a great deal of manhandling, and whilst his wife Marion may have given some assistance, it was probably left to the servants to do most of the fetching and carrying.

His second camera was a lightweight, hand-held instrument which allowed faster exposure times and greater mobility. Francis inadvertently photographed his own field camera whilst in Glenelg, for when using his hand held camera to photograph competitors in the Glenelg Highland Games he turned his lens toward fast moving dancers. On this 4 x 3 inch photograph in the album, we can see a field camera on a tripod standing unattended in the open space behind the dancers. *(91)*

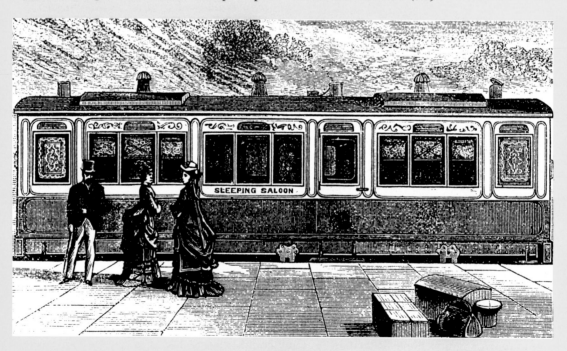

A drawing from a contemporary guide to Edinburgh showing a Sleeping-Car as used by the L.N.W.R.

The small camera recorded the high-jumpers, sack-racers, caber-tossers and reel-dancers in Glenelg, whilst the larger camera was used for over 160 of the photographs in the album, including the children with their driftwood at Nairn and that all important favourite image, the Tinker Woman.

Photography as a science, was just fifty years old in 1889 but great advances had been made, and the need to clamp the head of the sitter to stop him or her moving had long gone.

Fidgeting children could still be difficult to photograph however, as one Blair Atholl image shows; the family group posed in front of a door in the village have a small child seated on the step and the dear thing moved! *(34)* We do not even know if was a boy or girl.

But the view of Princes Street, Edinburgh, is full of movement that has been frozen in an instant of time. Even the penny-farthing rider and the young boy in the middle of the road, swinging his arms, have been recorded clearly. *(9)*

It is fortunate that Francis Smart, President of the Tunbridge Wells Amateur Photographic Association, was our traveller; he was a highly accomplished photographer, aware of every aspect of his art.

Rule 3 of his Association required *'that all Exhibits must be the work of the exhibitor – exposing, developing, re-touching, printing, toning and mounting...',* and dedicated camera club members throughout the British Isles still follow those rules today, although the growth of photo processing shops offering a 24 hour service, (some just one hour!), suggests that the majority of us have abandoned the dark-room for other pursuits. Francis, though, had an enquiring mind and would have enjoyed his time in the darkroom watching the negative images appearing on the glass plate.

Meanwhile, back in Aultbea, the couple stopped to enjoy a picnic but, try as we might, we could never find the exact site. *(45)*

Gairloch Hotel advertisement.

Secretly I was quite pleased because the photograph taken there was the most personal of all the ones taken in Scotland. Francis composed a picture, on the ground glass screen, of a coachman and a ladies' maid serving tea to his wife Marion. The coachman looked familiar and we checked back through the album. Sure enough we found him, sat in the driving seat of a coach outside the Loch Tummel Inn. *(27)*

But this could be no local man travelling the Highlands as a hired coachman. He has been allowed into the picture; he stares at the camera and is smiling because he is part of the family staff and enjoys the confidence of the photographer, his Master. He is quite youthful and one wonders if he was still in the employ of the family in 1913 when 22 members of the household staff attended the funeral of Francis Smart.

At Poolewe, whilst the coach waited on the road, Francis walked down to the river bank and recorded a familiar sight in the Highlands, women washing and trampling the clothes. *(47)* We visited the same spot on a beautiful summer day and only the women were missing; nothing else appeared to have changed in the last century.

Less than a mile from this spot are the famed Inverewe Gardens, created by Osgood MacKenzie from the early 1860s onwards and now in the care of the National Trust for Scotland.

On the panoramic view of Poolewe, Francis Smart's 1889 photograph shows the site with Mr. MacKenzie's large residence visible in the background. *(48)* Because of their great knowledge and interest in gardening, it is just conceivable that the Smarts had already written a letter of introduction to Osgood MacKenzie, and spent a few hours with him, looking at the progress made in the first 27 years of the project.

Alas, we will never know if that was so, but it is a pleasant thought.

But the couple had to move on and at Gairloch they boarded one of the regular paddle-steamers bound for Oban, calling at Portree, on the Isle of Skye, and Glenelg.

This west coast passenger trade was the virtual monopoly of one man, David MacBrayne, and his is still the most familiar name in all the Hebridean islands today. In 1889, from his office in Hope Street, Glasgow, he controlled a great fleet of ships including *'Columba'* and *'Iona'*, legends to this day.

Thirty-one other ships are listed in his brochure for this year and the Smarts took passage from Gairloch to Glenelg on the paddle steamer *'Mountaineer'*.

Photographs were taken from her and of her, and these appear in the album *(103 &*

The paddle steamer 'Mountaineer' as she looked a few days after she went aground off Lismore, September 1889. (Bob Charnley Collection).

104), but less than a month after their trip disaster struck! Inward bound from Glenelg to Oban, on 27 September, she ran aground in bad weather near the Lismore light. The passengers and crew were rescued but storms delayed the salvage work and she broke up and sank. A contemporary photograph in my collection (not taken by Francis Smart) shows the *'Mountaineer'* stranded on the rocks and still intact.

Two other problems still vexed the traveller, including no doubt the Smarts, in 1889; drivers' fees and pier dues.

'On one or two roads the former are abolished,' reported Mr. Baddeley in his guide, *'but the latter, most injudiciously imposed tax, maintains an evergreen vitality. The one is like paying an engine driver on a railway journey. The other, if not exactly on a par with paying for the use of a platform at a railway station, is as obsolete in theory as toll-gates.'* Ah, but they may yet return to Scotland! He continued, *'The fares on Scottish steamers are generally moderate, but as getting on and off are necessary parts of a steamboat journey, there is not the slightest excuse for putting the traveller to the annoyance of making two payments, or for employing two men when one would suffice.'*

Warming to his theme, Mr. Baddeley brings a flourishing conclusion to his 6th edition, 1889 Guide: *'Paterfamilias, all wreathed smiles as with a bag in one hand and a bundle of rugs in the other he sets foot on the gangway, is suddenly encountered by the lynx-eyed man at the gate, who demands twopence. What signifies it to our traveller that the pier belongs to the lord of the soil and not the steamboat company? His composure is upset for the next two hours, and then he goes home and abuses Scotland! These are minor drawbacks, and, to sum up, we hope that before long Scotland will be in all respects what it is in most; as good and as satisfactory a touring district as any in Europe.'*

STATION HOTEL,
OBAN, N.B.

The Only First-Class Hotel convenient to Railway Station and Pier.
BEAUTIFUL DINING AND DRAWING ROOMS. SPACIOUS WELL-VENTILATED SMOKING AND BILLIARD ROOMS.
Large Airy Bedrooms, handsomely furnished.
UNRIVALLED VIEWS.
C. CAMPBELL, *Proprietrix.*

An 1880s advertisement for the Station Hotel, Oban, the hotel used by the Smarts during their stay in the town.

Our own final journey in the footsteps of Francis and Marion was also to Oban; that delightful watering place on the west coast that we both know so very well, not least because we spent our honeymoon there some years ago now.

There is not an hour of the day, day of the week, or month of the year that I have not been in that town, in warm sunshine or driving rain and gale force winds; usually the latter when I have been making a winter crossing to Barra!

At any time the town is enjoyable and especially out of season, but when the couple reached Oban in September, 1889, it was the busiest week of the year. Visitors had already arrived from all over the world, evident from the lists of names and countries of origin that appeared in the local paper, the **'Oban Times'**. The reason for their presence was social. It was time for the Royal Highland Yacht Club Regatta and the Argyllshire Gathering and Games, and the bay was full of fine yachts with their rich Victorian gentlemen owners, families and friends, when the Smart family booked into the Station Hotel overlooking the scene. *(108)* The water and the boats attracted the attention of Francis and he recorded many fine images during the week or so that he and Marion spent in the town *(111)*.

Those who know Oban will have no problem identifying the sites of all the photographs, and many visitors have their own personal memories and photographs of twentieth century holidays and Gatherings in the town, just as we do.

Looking through the contemporary Victorian guide books one gets a great insight into the problems and the delights of the tourist in Scotland, and whilst the Smarts were not short of money they might have been continually influenced by Mr. Baddeley, whose famed guides helped many visitors world-wide.

'We have been at pains to collect tariffs from the favourite resorts of Scotland', he wrote in 1889, *'and have only found one instance in which the following is exceeded: Table d'hote Breakfast ...3s.0d.*
Table d'hote Dinner........4s.6d to 5s.0d.
Bed and Attendance.......from 4s.0d.

This scale rules at Edinburgh, Oban and Inverness, at all of which places 20 to 30 per cent may be saved by staying at smaller Temperance or partly Commercial houses, while in many country places the charges are somewhat lower. In small items, too, eatables and drinkables, an improvement has taken place, and visitors may, generally speaking, indulge in what is vulgarly called a 'snack' without paying the price of a full meal. This is, we hope, becoming universal.'

Now who would ever have thought that the word 'snack' was over a century old!

The same writer did not neglect the shipping companies and commented, favourably, *'The fare on the steamers is universally good, and the meals are served in simpler style; the tariff being, breakfast and tea 2 shillings, dinner 2/6d to 3 shillings.'* Well done MacBraynes. They still do good bacon *'snacks'!*

The old guide books were important tools in our quest and the flowery style of writing simply adds to our understanding of the age they relate to. They were well supported by their advertisers, packed with colour maps and free, up-to-date timetables, but they were relatively expensive if we make comparisons. In decimal coinage terms, dinner bed and breakfast cost 58 pence for a night at a hotel in 1889, as against an average of £25 in 1991. The two volumes of Mr. Baddeley's 1889 guides to Scotland cost 53 pence in decimal terms, a mere 5p less than the daily hotel rate.

Do many travellers to Scotland today pay around £25 for an annual guide to the country? Or do we rely on those wonderful productions from the various regions, the full colour accommodation guides, that are available for the price of a postage stamp?

Advertised on television, in the radio and television guides and the Sunday newspaper colour supplements at the start of each year, they have helped us to plan our tours in the footsteps of Francis and Marion and you must allow them to do the same for you. They will open up Scotland for both the first-time and the seasoned traveller, and they will guide you around the country as you record your own adventure, on film or video. Perhaps, in a later century, a fellow collector will discover your work on some dusty shelf!

CHAPTER FIVE

An Exhibition leads to a Great Discovery!

During the early part of 1989 Sandra and I made some plans for a major centenary exhibition of the photographs.

During the previous three years the pictures had been seen in Kingussie, Kintail and Glenelg, with a side-show for seven days at the Balmacara Hotel, near Kyle of Lochalsh. After that they were seen in England at Samlesbury Hall, a fourteenth-century manor house in Lancashire, mid-way between Preston and Blackburn, and the attentions of Granada Television attracted the public to visit the exhibition in their thousands.

At all these venues we had an opportunity to assess public interest, vary the range of pictures on display, and improve the captions, and having a collection of Victorian guide books for reference was useful for the latter.

No doubt the Smarts had read about the places they would be visiting in advance of their tour and I am sure they would have purchased a copy of the 1889 edition of Mr. M.J.B. Baddeley's *'Guide to Scotland'*. It included thirty-seven maps and plans and a copy of the annual rail, coach and steamer fare and timetables for the 1889 season. This Victorian guide-book reveals a different pace of life, and the five hour journey by coach for the 28 miles from Achnasheen to Gairloch in 1889, is just the time it takes to reach Oban from our home, 300 miles and a century away!

Late in October, 1988, we received tentative approaches from the National Library of Scotland in Edinburgh, when a letter arrived from Dr. Kenneth Gibson, the Exhibition Officer, suggesting that space might be available at the end of the following year for a major exhibition of the photographs of *the anonymous photographer'*.

It had always been our intention to have a showing during the centenary year and I had hoped to return to Glenelg, a place that had obviously captivated the photographer judging from the great number of pictures that were taken there.

Sandra, though, argued that space was needed if we were to do justice to the pictures and whilst Glenelg had the peace, Edinburgh had the space, especially for pictures up to 48 inches wide. Furthermore, whilst village halls are readily available it is not so easy to find prestigious space in Edinburgh for three months and reach a new and larger audience. I agreed.

It took me a long time to realize that twelve months to plan an exhibition is too short a period. We were skilled in setting up and dismantling a display in hours at village halls and galleries, but this was to be no small scale affair and the Trustees of the National Library of Scotland are due unqualified praise for the work of Kenny Gibson and his faithful assistant Jackie Cromarty.

What they achieved, with the seventy-five pictures we supplied, was a stunning, well lit display of the images, with easy to read captions and an informative leaflet. My friendly technical wizard, Mike Day, put in a great many hours in the darkroom, working with the large amount of photographic paper generously donated by John Barker, the Managing Director of Kentmere Limited, of Staveley in Cumbria, who were acting as sponsors of the exhibition. Most people will not worry what sort of paper their holiday photos are printed on as long as they look good. But we had the advantage of being able to study 100 year old, sepia originals and it was important that they be matched, as closely as possible, to the tones achieved by Francis Smart.

The paper we chose gave just that quality, and the resulting prints were universally praised and admired by the public.

Titled *'The Summer of '89',* the exhibition was opened by one of Scotland's leading landscape photographers, Colin Baxter, whose studies are readily available on postcard everywhere.

It is my opinion that these are the postcard collector's items of the future and should be avidly purchased and saved. The financial outlay is so small that the youngest child can start a collection that will be the envy of many of his middle-aged friends in AD 2040.

By invitation some 150 people attended the opening evening on the first day of December and there were renewed meetings with many friends who made the trip to Edinburgh that day. It was especially a pleasure to be able to greet people who had Glenelg 'connections' and who had seen the very first public showing in the village hall, and in particular the lady who had asked to see the album in Glenelg village hall (and was initially refused), Dr. Ann Matheson!

Behind the scenes Kenny Gibson had prepared a press release with the bold heading **'Clever Detective Work Exposes Victorian Photographer'** and it did the trick. But then doesn't everybody love a good mystery story!

The newspaper, television and radio coverage that the exhibition received – including a second appearance with Jimmie Macgregor (remember the singing duo Robin Hall and Jimmie Macgregor?) on his morning radio show – was quite enormous and continued until the final week of February, when the event closed.

The photographs were highly acclaimed by the critics and the public responded. Staff at the National Library had indicated that a good attendance figure for a winter show might be around 1000 people each month. The final figure exceeded 9500 and two, very full, visitor's books record the praise that the photographer deserves.

The world is a small place now but it is heartening to see that the tourists do not neglect Scotland in winter. Apart from the North American visitors and the Europeans (with the notable exception of the French), the books contain names and addresses of visitors from Malaya, Singapore and Hong Kong, Japan, Australia and New Zealand, Turkey, South Africa and Zimbabwe.

Then letters also started to arrive, not just from the public but from book publishers, postcard companies and a bank, and three leisure centres who wanted to take the exhibition over when it closed down. As for the pictures themselves, they were to be moved to the Landmark Highland Heritage & Adventure Park at Carrbridge, Invernessshire, at the end of the exhibition and be on public display until 1993.

Some sixteen of the best images have been reproduced on postcard and are generally available at the Publications Counter of the National Library, Landmark Centre and elsewhere in Scotland.

And that was it!

The promise of a Centenary Exhibition had been fulfilled and now was the time to relax, enjoy a special Christmas with Sandra overlooking the Isle of Skye, and partake of good meals with friends. It should have been all over but there was one more, big, surprise still to come!

At the Edinburgh exhibition the caption under the photograph of the Tinker Woman in Glenelg read:

> *'..The haunting, enquiring look in her eyes has been recorded on the photographic plate and is now seen by more people than either the photographer or the subject could have imagined. Sadly we may never know her name or what became of the children, who could possibly have lived through two world wars and survived into the second half of the 20th century.'*

One evening in January, 1990, some five weeks after the start of the exhibition and now back at home, we were just settling down to watch the 6 o'clock BBC News, with an early evening meal, when the telephone rang. I picked up the receiver.

It was Domhnall MacCormaig, a distinguished antiquarian book dealer in Edinburgh whose speciality is Celtic Studies and Scottish History.

'Hello Bob. Now how would you like to know the name of the Tinker Woman?' he asked. I hesitated, my heart thumping madly. I suspected my leg was about to be pulled however gently. But perhaps Domhnall really *had* discovered something.

'Go on,' I urged. 'I'm listening!'

'Well I won't give you the name myself,' he said, tauntingly. 'But I can put you in touch with someone who will!'

Then a conversation took place that I cannot repeat because my recollection of those few minutes has gone.

I remember listening to Domhnall as he talked about some of his relatives who thought they knew the name of the Tinker Woman because of a family likeness, but really I was thinking about the impact that the name would have and frantically searching for a pencil all at the same time. The television was on, I couldn't reach the remote-control button and the tea tray was sliding off my knee. It really was all a bit sudden!

I wouldn't have wanted it any other way however! A fax would have been impersonal and a letter less urgent.

I made a note, on the back of a scrap of paper, of the name and telephone number of the person who would give me all the details, rather puzzled by the area code which began with 087. I knew that it belonged to the Barra and Uists

Tinker Woman at Glenelg.

area of the Western Isles but I could see no obvious connection with that Glenelg photograph. After I had thanked Domhnall and replaced the receiver I turned back to my tea; it was stone cold!

Thousands of leaflets, with the Tinker Woman on the front cover, had been printed for the exhibition by Her Majesty's Stationery Office in Edinburgh, and with the image regularly appearing in newspapers and on the television, many people who were unable to visit Edinburgh at least saw some of the photographs.

Up around Beauly a lady, having connections with travelling people, thought she saw a family likeness in the Tinker Woman. She, in turn, contacted other members of her family who agreed. The word spread quickly and reached the ears of Domhnall who passed on the information to me. The Western Isles phone number that I had been given belonged to one of the female relatives who was prepared to talk to me.

Not wishing to be publicly identified and understanding her personal reasons, I will call this lady *Fiona*.

After a couple of attempts I managed to catch Fiona at home and I introduced myself down the telephone line, listening intently to her beautiful, soft, Hebridean lilt as she spoke.

'Please tell me a little about yourself,' I urged, realizing that the information I wanted might be very personal and not what one might wish to reveal to a complete stranger over the phone.

Fiona quietly, but proudly, told me of her early life, explaining how she came from a long line of travelling people and had spent all of her own youth moving around the countryside.

I asked about her present situation and she told me she was married with a family and lived in a house in the Outer Hebrides.

Like all travelling people throughout the world the Scottish travellers, or tinkers, have their oral traditions which pass through the generations. Seldom written down, the stories run the risk of being corrupted with the passage of time, but the main thread is usually there.

'Henny'

Fiona told me how she was related to a family of travellers, or more correctly 'tinsmiths', whose territory one hundred years ago was part of Skye, Glenelg and the village of Arnisdale on Loch Hourn. The female line of this family came from the Hebridean island of Lewis.

In the last half of the nineteenth century travelling tinsmiths Charles and Janet Stewart had two daughters; Henny, and Bella who was born in Balallan, Lewis, in March 1865.

Henny, who according to Fiona was some fifteen years younger than Bella, travelled with her elder sister around the Glenelg area but when she was only 25 years old, Henny apparently slipped whilst crossing a river near Arnisdale, a village 13 miles south of Glenelg, was swept away and drowned.

Seeing the picture of the Tinker Woman with a young girl by her side and detecting a family likeness the present generation made contact with each other, and in true Sherlock Holmes fashion certain deductions were made!

I promised Fiona a good copy of the photograph of the Tinker Woman so that it could be passed around the family, and I resolved to tackle the records of births, marriages and deaths for Scotland, held at the General Register Office in Edinburgh, in an effort to trace the family.

Over a period of some weeks I made regular trips to the capital searching the files and then checking and rechecking the facts with Fiona over the telephone. Determining the correct names of the sisters was slow work at first, especially as the registers are full of people with the surname of Stewart, but I eventually found that on 21 June, 1898, 18 year old Henny (christened Henrietta) Stewart, daughter of Charles and Janet, travelling tinsmiths, married 17 year old John Stewart, son of tinsmiths Peter and Henny, at Bunessan on the Isle of Mull. Her sad end came on 14 October, 1905, at 6 p.m. at Glen Arnisdale, Dr. Campbell from Glenelg certifying the cause as *death by drowning*.

An enquiry took place and the Procurator Fiscal's Office in Inverness confirmed the cause of death two weeks later.

Henny Stewart was buried close to the wall in the tiny cemetery by the sea, in Arnisdale village. I visited the unmarked grave with Eddie Stiven, very soon after obtaining the information, and talked to two local men, Iain MacKenzie and Archie McLean.

They confirmed Fiona's version of Henny's death; a sad episode still remembered in the village, the story having been passed on down through the generations.

Indeed Archie told me how his father had made a wooden cross for the grave in 1905 and that it was only within the last few years that it had rotted away leaving the spot unmarked today.

Later that day, sitting in front of the fire in his cottage overlooking Loch Hourn, Archie turned to me and said quietly 'Was she related to *Beileag an Tin* then?'

I looked at him with a puzzled frown; I don't have the Gaelic you understand!

He smiled sadly, remembering that he had an Englishman in his house.

'Bella', he said patiently. 'Was she a relative of Bella of the Tin?'

'Yes Archie, I'm sure she was!'

He didn't reply. I waited. Nothing. The rain was starting to patter on the window pane; the light of that February day was fading fast and we had to get back to Glenelg before dark.

As I shook his hand and thanked him, Archie just said 'Aye, Bella. All the old people used to know of Bella around here.' His thoughts were obviously far away.

Official records show that Henny's elder sister Bella, who was christened Isabella and came from the Isle of Lewis, married 23 year old Alexander MacDonald, son of John and Mary, travelling tinsmiths, on 18 May, 1885, at Portree, Skye, and on 22 April, 1889, she gave birth to a son, Solomon.

Donning my Holmes deer-stalker I was able to make my own deductions about the Mona Lisa of Francis Smart's photograph and concluded that she was *indeed* Isabella MacDonald. The clues?

Francis Smart's photographs, as we know, were taken in the summer of 1889 and the Tinker Woman with the baby is outside a croft in Glenelg.

Sisters Henny and Bella were nine and twenty-four year-olds in 1889, and Bella had given birth to a son, Solomon, in April that year, as the records in Edinburgh confirmed.

I knew from the descendants of the family, and now Archie McLean in Arnisdale, that Glenelg was part of the territory which Bella travelled in, and where she called on the crofters selling her pails and other utensils.

The girls' and the baby's apparent age in the 1889 photograph fit those of Henny, Bella and Solomon in the same year.

In that picture taken by Francis in August, 1889, nine year old Henny is standing next to her elder married sister Isabella MacDonald, who has her young son Solomon slung on her back. *(98)* All three are outside the 1889 home of Alex and Mary McLeod at Quarry, Glenelg, now the site of the house where Mr. and Mrs. Stiven live with their son Calum, who was born exactly one hundred years to the month after baby Solomon.

A coincidence indeed, made more amazing when one recalls how Donna, Eddie and I uncovered the clues within the walls of the same house. What discoveries we made that day!

Whilst I was gathering details of the Stewart girls, in February, 1990, I had reason to talk on the telephone to a lady living in the Borders. She had visited the exhibition at the National Library and given the leaflet, with the Tinker Woman on the cover, to her husband, who was from a travelling family. She told me of his reaction to the photograph.

'If that is Glenelg,' he had said to his wife, 'that woman is a MacDonald from Skye.'

Neither of them had any idea that search was on, or that the MacDonald connection had been uncovered.

During the summer of 1990, Sandra and I were touring the Outer Hebrides when we landed on the island where Fiona lived.

'I would love to meet Fiona personally and thank her for all her help.' I said to Sandra. 'Let's drive over there one day.'

'Can you remember the address?'

'Not off hand but I have the phone number.' I replied.

And so, on the following Saturday afternoon, whilst driving in the district, I pulled up at a lonely, rain-swept telephone box and rang.

Fiona's husband answered and I told him where we were.

'You're just a few minutes away,' he said. 'Come on up to the house!'

When we arrived he explained that Fiona had gone off to the local Highland Games with their daughter who was competing in some of the events.

'If you are going there, look out for a Peugeot car on the road. She's bound to be coming back home for something or other!' he said, with a laugh. We chatted for a few minutes and then took our leave.

The rain was being driven by a strong wind now and visibility was poor. I turned the car headlights on and continued towards the *machair* where the games were being held. On a straight stretch of single track road a car appeared out of the gloom some one hundred yards away. The nearest passing place was on my side of the road and I pulled in, dipping my lights as I did so.

It was a Peugeot with a lady driver. I flashed my lights, waved her down and she stopped alongside me. Through the open car windows, sandwiching the wind and the rain, I held out a postcard of the Tinker Woman and offered it to her.

'I'm Bob Charnley and you must be Fiona. Nice to meet you at last!' I said, with a triumphant grin. She appeared surprised.

'Yes, er..yes? But how did you know?' she replied, a puzzled look on her face.

'Hello, hello! This is lovely!' she continued, her dark eyes darting between our faces and then down to the postcard I had just handed to her. Now she was smiling and relaxed. The picture of Isabella had finally brought us together.

Later, the same afternoon, we walked around the games field together, the smell of fried onions drifting along with the drizzle from the direction of the catering tent; a piper, in the shelter of a sand dune, playing a lament. The biting, swirling wind blew his tune away.

Fiona talked again of her childhood, the ways of the travelling people in the Highlands and Islands and of the Stewart girls in the 1889 photograph, and I realised I was in the presence of a true champion for her cause.

I do hope she will pass on her great knowledge and enthusiasm for the travellers to future generations, for they deserve greater recognition and understanding from the majority of us who perhaps misunderstood their role in Highland society.

Fiona, thank you for all your help! I made you a promise when we had that first telephone conversation and I have kept the secret you shared with me.

The Highland tinkers were a part of the community in the 1880s; today most of those who remain out on the road are *apart*.

When Francis and Marion visited Glenelg the tinkers provided a great service in the area and the same piece of land was made available for their camp, year in, year out. That particular spot was photographed by Francis Smart and it shows evidence of being both home and a work-place for the family; a chicken scratches around the tent and pieces of tin litter the ground and wall. *(76)*

Home was easily built, and just as easily dismantled. Long branches of birch, or hazel, were placed upright in the ground, usually in an oval form. The tops were bent across and tied together forming the required shape of an upturned boat. The tarpaulin was thrown across, held down by ropes or with heavy stones resting on the base, and the home was ready. The men in the family did the manufacturing and repair work on a variety of items, from the humble tea-spoon to the much used water pail, whilst the women went around the village soliciting repair work and selling the finished products.

To a remote Highland village community they were important people, providing a useful service and a link with other communities further afield. Often it would be the travelling families who would bring news of national importance to these villages. Those days have gone, but the travellers still exist in their world *apart*.

The fault is not of their making for this century has left them behind. For present day

A typical travellers' camp about the turn of the century. (Copyright Inverness Museum & Art Gallery).

requirements they tend to use a car or, more usually, a van with plenty of load carrying capacity; but should you be driving between Castle Stalker and Ballachulish, along the shores of Loch Linnhe, you may well see the same tarpaulin home as in the photograph, alongside the modern vehicle. There are still some travellers unwilling or unable to severe the links with the past.

Our quest, of course, is far from completed, as indeed each image invokes a personal story of its own. If bringing the album to a wider audience triggers recognition in a reader who might be able to add further to the meagre store of knowledge so far gleaned, please let us know. And especially the people of Tunbridge Wells, and elsewhere in Kent, and Combe Hay, who may hold keys to the whereabouts of other photographs taken by this gifted man, Francis Smart.

CHAPTER SIX

The Private Lives of the Smart Family

By the end of the summer months of 1990 I thought we had finished our search for the people and the places seen by Francis and Marion during their summer tour of Scotland. Yet, as I sat reading the 1913 newspaper obituary report one September evening, I realized that something was missing about the man himself, and I had overlooked it first time around.

Francis was a fully qualified doctor, as was his father, yet throughout the entire obituary notice in the *'Kent and Sussex Courier'* he was referred to as Mr. Francis Smart and no mention was made of his qualification. That omission bothered me and there was a need to know the reason for it, so I decided to travel to Scarborough, their family home, and revisit Tunbridge Wells, hoping to satisfy my curiosity.

The Smart family had their roots in the north east of England; in Scarborough, Yorkshire. Francis's grandfather, Dr. George Smart, was born in Hutton Buscel, near Scarborough, in the year 1791, and became a surgeon. His father, John Cass Smart, was born in the same village in 1815 but, by 1844, John and his wife Mabel were in Leeds when their first child Francis Gray was born. In the early 1850s the family had moved back to the coast and were living in Ashburn Villa, Valley Road, Scarborough, a building commissioned by Dr. John, whose medical practice was at 8, Huntriss Row at this time.

In the 1860s the Smarts disappear from Scarborough records; they had apparently moved to London where the father had taken up a post as a homoeopathic specialist, but by 1871 the family were in Tunbridge Wells as the entry in *'Kelly's Directory for Kent'* confirms: *'John Cass Smart, Belvedere House, Tunbridge Wells., Physician.'* In the *Kelly's* for 1882, however, the entry reads: *'Francis Gray Smart M.A., M.B.Cantab., Physician, and John Cass Smart M.D., Physician. Belvedere House, Church Road, Tunbridge Wells.'* At this time Belvedere House was a very large property with extensive gardens at the corner of Church Road but the building was demolished later and a cinema erected on the site.

It is quite evident, from newspaper reports, that both doctors were highly esteemed in the town and ran a thriving practice, although by 1882 Dr. John was approaching his seventieth year and the bulk of the work was falling on the shoulders of the young Dr. Francis who was still in his thirties. But the older, established patients still remained the responsibility of the father and it was one of his patients who was to have a great effect on the entire Smart family.

Here I must introduce Mr. Thomas Jones Gibb of Tunbridge Wells, described as *'a merchant prince'* in the local paper.

Born in 1821 he had spent most of his active life in China amassing a large fortune in the silk trade and on his return trips to England he frequented Tunbridge Wells. Sometime around 1867, at the age of 46, Mr. Jones Gibb decided to live in the town and purchased four properties on a site called Mount Ephraim. Having cleared the site he built a beautiful mansion, called it 'Bredbury', and when adjoining properties came on the market he purchased them too. Because of his *'immense wealth'* he apparently spared no expense in turning 'Bredbury' into a palatial residence and *'everything thought of that could be suggested in the shape of improvement was immediately done'*.

Indeed the very size of the house and grounds meant that at least twelve full-time indoor staff and gardeners were required.

But whilst they used their personal wealth for the benefit of themselves and their servants, both Mr. and Mrs. Jones Gibb gave greatly to charitable institutions during their married life together, most of the churches in Tunbridge Wells benefiting from their munificence. Also receiving support was the General Hospital, the Mansion House funds, the Mechanics' Institute and many, many other causes.

At Christmas, it was said, he *'dispensed his bounty with a very generous hand'*, and regularly defrayed the costs of the teas and treats for the school-children, as well as suppers for the deserving poor. But however large his charity in Tunbridge Wells, and large it certainly was, he also supported *'many well known institutions and benevolent agencies in the metropolis'*. It is right to add that it was only with his death in 1884 that Jones Gibb's charity became widely known. Previously only those privileged to dispense his bounty had any certain knowledge of the source of it all.

But Thomas Jones Gibb entered his sixties in poor health, brought about, it was said, by his continual exposure to the climate in China earlier in life and for the last few years of his life he was a virtual invalid.

A small, turn of the century, book about the Tunbridge Wells General Hopital contained this photograph of Mrs. Marion Smart. This chance discovery by Jean Mauldon, Reference Librarian at the Central Library in Tunbridge Wells, was of great value. It allowed positive identification of Marion Smart as the lady photographed by Francis at the picnic near Aultbea in August 1989 and outside the manor at Combe Hay at the end of the tour.

His family physician, Dr. John Cass Smart, was a regular visitor to 'Bredbury', but at the beginning of July, 1884, he was called to the house because of a serious change in the condition of his patient and within a short time a *'disease of the kidneys'* was diagnosed. Despite the constant, unremitting attention of the doctor, Thomas Jones Gibb's condition deteriorated and *'little hope was entertained of his recovery'*. On the morning of Friday 11th July, 1884, in his sixty third year, he peacefully passed away. He left a 53 year old widow.

Because of the large number of mourners at the funeral the cortege left 'Bredbury' some thirty minutes later than planned that July afternoon.

The funeral carriage was drawn by four magnificent jet black horses followed by the private carriage of the widow. In all twenty-seven carriages assembled behind the coffin which was heaped with *'wreathes and crosses composed of choice and beautiful white flowers and ferns'*, and in the sixth carriage sat the Rev. G. Jones with the family physician, Dr. John Cass Smart. Behind them, in the next carriage, came the Rev. J.H. Townsend, vicar of St.Mark's, Tunbridge Wells, who was the officiating clergyman, with Dr. Francis at his side.

Four of the other carriages brought the staff from 'Bredbury' including the butler, head gardener, five gardeners, a groom and four female domestic servants, and as the bells of St.Peter's Church were tolled, Thomas Jones Gibb was laid to rest in the New

Cemetery, Tunbridge Wells, in a vault which had been prepared and ready for some two years. A vast crowd witnessed those final moments, but within the vault itself few saw the widow as she placed her own personal wreath on the coffin as it was lowered to the ground.

Probate of the will was granted to Mrs. Jones Gibb on 2 August, 1884, and Thomas left instructions that his wife receive *'£2,000 for her immediate use..'* to be paid as soon as possible after his death, together with 'Bredbury' and entire contents; land and property in Bickley Park, Kent and elsewhere. The St. Marks Hospital, City Road, London, received £2,000 with gifts of £1,000 to each of eight other hospitals. Trust funds were created for some eighteen relatives and friends ranging in value from £20,000 through £10,000 and £5,000 down to £1,000, the latter including *'Francis Gray Smart of Belvedere House, Tunbridge Wells, aforesaid Doctor of Medicine'.*

The total value of these trusts was £86,000 but for his wife he set aside a trust of *'£100,000 absolutely for her own use and benefits'* plus the surplus of the residuary estate. The total of the known sum, trusts and legacies, exceeded £200,000, a figure worth around £6 million in 1991 terms.

Eighteen months passed by; and then, on 12th January, 1886, at Holy Trinity Church, Paddington, London, the Chaplain to Her Majesty Queen Victoria, the Rev. Daniel Moore MA., assisted by the Rev. R.T.W. Brayne MA., joined Dr. Francis Gray Smart MA., MB., in marriage to Mrs. Marion Jones Gibb of 'Bredbury', Tunbridge Wells.

Obviously taken by surprise, the **'Kent and Sussex Courier'** reported that *'the marriage of this benevolent lady, whose name has become a household word in the town, will no doubt be read with interest by a very wide circle of friends and those to whom she is known by her good deeds. As the marriage was of a private character we are not in a position to give further details, but we may mention that the newly united couple have gone for a lengthened tour on the Continent.'*

For personal reasons the quiet wedding took place in London, Mrs. Jones Gibb, now Mrs. Smart, marrying from the home of her mother.

At last the pieces of the puzzle were beginning to fit together. A successful doctor marries the widow of one of his father's patients and quite simply retires from his practice.

Doctor Francis Smart became plain Mister Smart and spent the rest of his life devoting himself to scientific, photographic, botanical and charitable pursuits.

The 1904 edition of a local book about prominent worthies, **'Kent-Contemporary Biographies',** confirms this with the statement that *'Francis Smart practised in Tunbridge Wells for some years, and retired eighteen years ago'.* This would be in 1886, the year of his marriage to Marion.

How opportune that the doctor who received £1,000 in the will of Thomas Jones Gibb and had hoped, perhaps, to attend the widow in a medical capacity, should end up marrying the rich lady, 13 years his senior!

At the same time that Francis was getting married, his 71 year old father, Dr. John Smart, was retiring. He left Tunbridge Wells for Combe Hay near Bath, a small village with a population of 184 people at this time.

There he has purchased the magnificent, early eighteenth-century manor house with extensive grounds and with the help of his family, especially son George Edward, he tends a herd of pedigree Jersey cows. *(121)* Sadly, on a July day in 1894, whilst away from Combe Hay visiting his sister in Scarborough, he collapsed in the street outside the shop of an old friend and died within minutes. He was 79 years old.

Meanwhile back in Tunbridge Wells, at 8.30 p.m. on 20 January, 1887, a group of men meet at the home of a Mr. J.G. Calway. They resolve to form a Photographic Club and, after some discussion, agree that it be called the Tunbridge Wells Amateur Photographic Association and that *'Francis Smart be asked to become first President of the Association.'* He accepts and the rest is history. His professional colleagues, amongst them Henry Peach Robinson the great Victorian photographer, admire his talents with the camera and within the Association he receives many prizes, including the *'Amateur Photographer Magazine'* Bronze Medal and Sir David Salomons', Bart., Medal.

In 1890 the Association made arrangements with the South of England Telephone Company for an exchange to be erected inside the Sussex Assembly Rooms, where their annual photographic exhibition was being held, and visitors were encouraged to come in and use the instrument.

Out of a total population of about 29,000 Tunbridge Wells had just under 100 telephone subscribers in 1890, so it was still a great novelty for the general public. The company, naturally, was hoping that the caller would talk to a local telephone owner and be persuaded to subscribe himself, but my sympathies are with the owners who kept receiving unnecessary phone calls all week! I hope they received a reward for their patience.

A century has now passed, and from Tunbridge Wells today I can transmit a copy of Francis Smart's photograph, as on the cover, down the telephone line to a friend in the remote Highland village of Glenelg. In under one minute she will be looking at the Tinker Woman who walked within yards of her cottage one hundred years ago.

In 1891 Francis added two more Silver and two further Bronze Medals to his collection and the *'Tunbridge Wells Advertiser'*, reporting on the annual exhibition,

A wonderful 'spread' prepared by the Smart's household staff at 'Bredbury' for the members of the Photographic Association who visited their President at his home, August, 1908. (Photo courtesy Tunbridge Wells Library Collection)

The beautiful mansion 'Bredbury' on Mount Ephraim, Tunbridge Well, the home of Francis and Marion Smart from 1886 until their deaths in 1913. (Photo courtesy Tunbridge Wells Library Collection).

noted that:

'Mr. F.G. Smart, the President, is the most numerous local exhibitor. And that is not all, for, to prove that quality can go with quantity, these pictures came to the front for their superiority of treatment; the results, perhaps, not only of good taste and study, but also of means and leisure, which are two possessions that take one a considerable distance along the road to success in this somewhat expensive hobby.' Perhaps Francis agreed with the 'means and leisure' remark but his personal attitude to the hobby is revealed in his opening statement at the 1891 Exhibition when he exhorted his fellow members to *'Amuse the townsmen, keep our own work up to the mark, and try and interest others in an art which we find so fascinating.'*

In November, 1904, the Tunbridge Wells Amateur Photographic Association instituted a 'one man show' and from the fifty-five strong membership an invitation was sent to the President, Francis Smart.

His exhibition lasted for ten days and whilst no complete record of his exhibits could be found, the photographs were mostly 12 x 10 inches and comprised *'landscapes, seascapes, figure studies and architecture, which goes to show the multiplicity of work done by this gentleman, several having gained awards'.* A meagre list in the local paper mentions *'Yachts at Oban'* which he may have photographed during his 1889 'Scotch Tour', but I was left in no doubt that Francis returned to Scotland when I saw *'Aberdeen Harbour'* and *'Kilpick Church, on the Clunie, Braemar'* in the list. So now we have another quest!

But in March, 1913, the staff at 'Bredbury', and the townspeople of Tunbridge Wells, were devastated by the news that Marion had died. Whilst everyone was aware that

57

Francis was seriously ill, no one was prepared for the sudden death of his wife.

On the afternoon of Thursday, 27 March, she had visited her husband in his sickroom and satisfied herself that his nurse had made him comfortable. That was the last time they saw each other. On the Friday Marion underwent a *'serious operation'* from which she never rallied but passed away peacefully on the afternoon of Saturday, 29 March, 1913, aged 82 years.

Francis lasted only a little longer. Just after midnight on Monday, 7 April. 1913 he died at the age of 69 years.

Because of their secretive approach to charitable causes Francis and Marion covered their tracks but their known charity was considerable during their twenty seven years of married life. In 1903, for example, Francis donated the sum of £6,500 to the Homoeopathic Hospital in Tunbridge Wells and in 1911 he gave a further four figure sum to the same hospital. It will never be possible to compile a list of all their donations, nor would they have wanted it done, but it was public knowledge that the Smarts gave money to the R.N.L.I. and Heather Deane, the Deputy Public Relations Officer at R.N.L.I. Headquarters, Poole, kindly unearthed the following pieces of information.

In 1879 Marion, and her first husband Thomas, paid for the 30 foot, 8 oar Life-boat *'Tom and Marion'* at Blyth, Northumberland.

In 1885, after the death of Thomas Jones Gibb, Marion purchased the 37 foot, 12 oar Life-boat *'The Jones Gibb'*, which went to Barmouth, and in her will of 1913 she left the sum of £2,000 for the Institution.

That legacy was used in 1926, when at Yarmouth, Isle of Wight, His Royal Highness The Prince of Wales named the 45 foot "Watson" (Motor) Life-boat *'B.A.S.P.'* after the first letter of the surnames of the donors, for by this period the cost of a boat was around £7,500 and the money from four legacies, including that of Marion, was needed for the purchase.

But it was as husband and wife in 1886, the first year of their married life, that Francis and Marion gifted a Life-boat and the following report appeared in the *'Life-boat Journal'* in November of that year:

> *'Newquay, Cardiganshire, and this Station has received one of the new 37 feet 12 oared Life-boats, the gift of Mr. and Mrs. FRANCIS G. SMART of Tunbridge Wells, the boat bearing their joint names, 'The Frank and Marion'. This is the third Life-boat that Mrs. SMART has presented to the Institution. On the occasion of the first launch of the new Life-boat, on the 23rd September, the whole town of Newquay kept holiday, and the inhabitants, as well as those of the district for miles round, turned out to witness the proceedings-a most enthusiastic reception being extended to the donors who were present...'.*

Here the *'Journal'* quotes in full the address given by the Reverend D Griffiths in which he thanks the donors and continues, *'It is a subject of deep thankfulness that the calls of the Institution are so liberally met throughout the length and breadth of the land. God, the Father of all, puts it into the hearts of ladies and gentlemen such as you, who are endowed with wealth, to think of the perils and dangers of those our brothers whose work lies, and whose lives are spent, on the sea...'*

Then, adds the *'Journal'*, Mr. Smart *'appropriately acknowledged the receipt of the address, and said that it gave him and his wife great pleasure to be present, and that they felt very gratified at the cordial and warm reception afforded them. A short religious service was then conducted by the*

Rev. D. GRIFFITHS, after which the ceremony of naming the boat was performed by Mrs. SMART, who broke the customary wine-bottle over the stern, when the boat glided into the water amid vociferous cheering of the crowds.

The donors afterwards caused tea to be provided for the Life-boatmen and their wives and a number of aged persons, as well as for 550 school children. On leaving Newquay they were waited on by the Life-boat crew, and Mr. GRIFFITH THOMAS, the second coxswain, who expressed their sincerest and warmest thanks for their great liberality.'

Marion also left around £36,000 for distribution to various hospitals, missions or homes, including the Homoeopathic hospitals in London and Tunbridge Wells. A codicil to the will added £10,000 for the Tunbridge Wells hospital to provide a *'Frank Smart'* wing and on 29 June 1921 Her Royal Highness Princess Louise, Duchess of Argyll, performed the opening ceremony. Marion's legacy went a very long way towards the total of £11,000 that the building actually cost.

The bulk of the estate went to nephews Thomas Jones Gibb Duncanson of Hadlow House, Uckfield, Essex, Edward Ford Duncanson of Nutwood, Bickley Park, Kent, and various other Duncanson wives or children. In fact over £250,000 in legacies and trust funds went to the Duncansons.

But to Thomas Jones Gibb Duncanson went the lion's share. Apart from a £100,000 legacy he also received the 'Bredbury' estate with all *'furniture, plate, linen, glass, china, pictures, ornaments, carriages, implements and other effects'*, and other properties and land in Tunbridge Wells.

All this was possible because Marion had retained control of everything her first husband had passed on to her; there was no joint ownership of 'Bredbury' with her husband Francis, although her will gave him *'during his life, the personal use and occupation of my freehold dwellinghouse....called 'Bredbury' at Mount Ephraim..'.* The value of the trusts and legacies in Marion's will exceeded £390,000, or in 1991 terms *£7.6 million.*

Thomas Jones Gibb Duncanson was born in 1873, educated at Harrow and Emmanuel College, Cambridge (B.A., M.A.) where he was awarded a rowing 'blue'. He served as a Lieutenant in the R.N.V.R. during the Great War and died in 1933.

The central figure of our story, Francis Gray Smart, was equally as generous in that he bequeathed or provided trust funds which exceeded £310,000, a figure of around *£6 million* in 1991 terms.

To his brother George Edward at Combe Hay, Bath, he left £60,000 cash or the option of stocks and shares to that value, together with *'my two cottages, Orchard, watercress bed and hereditaments adjoining the Rectory Gardens at Combe Hay'*, and a codicil added a further £5,000 legacy in addition to the figure already mentioned.

For his sister Margaret he set up a £35,000 trust fund and left her most of his books.

Each of the Homoeopathic hospitals in London and Tunbridge Wells received £10,000 and the sum of £5,000 went to the United Kingdom Beneficent Association to found a *'Frank Smart'* pension for Protestant, male, British Subjects.

In addition he supported the Protestant Alliance with a gift of £2,000 and made it quite clear to his trustees that should any beneficiary become Roman Catholic before they received the money then 80% must be withdrawn and passed on *'to any Protestant Society which will be most useful in opposing the spread of Romanism'.*

As I purchased the 'Scotch Tour' album legitimately I do not intend to have my 80% withdrawn at this late date!

But the greatest sums, once again, went to the Duncanson families. Trusts and legacies to the various members exceeded £70,000 and with the benefits received from Marion the total monetary value of these bequests was around the £325,000 figure.

To Edward Ford Duncanson went the books on Architecture and Archaeology from his library and *'all my cameras, lenses and photographic apparatus and materials'*.

To Thomas Jones Gibb Duncanson went *'My collection of British and English coins'* and to his own sister Margaret four watches, but *'not either of the watches which belonged to Queen Elizabeth and Queen Anne respectively, and I bequeath the remainder of the same collection, including the two watches which belonged to Queen Elizabeth and Queen Anne, to the Fitzwilliam Museum, Cambridge, on condition that they be placed and kept in a separate case and labelled as the "Frank Smart" benefaction'*.

Enquiries at the Fitzwilliam Museum received a prompt reply from the Assistant Keeper of Applied Art, Miss Julia Poole, on behalf of the Keeper, Robin Crighton.

'I have checked our catalogue of the Smart Collection,' she wrote. 'There are no references to a watch belonging to Queen Elizabeth I, although there are several late sixteenth-century watches. The watch by Thuilet has the royal arms used by Queen Anne after 1707 engraved roughly on the inner cover. The collection comprises 104 watches and is generally held to be a fine one.'

Both Marion and Francis Smart's wills contain some personal touches.

To their physician, Dr. Neild of Tunbridge Wells, they left sums totalling £1,500 and whilst Francis remembered one of the clergymen who married them in 1886, the Rev. R.T.W. Brayne, who received a £2,000 legacy with a further £500 for his youngest son, Marion bequeathed *'to my friend Miss E. Alice Buckle of Tunbridge Wells, free of legacy duty, the sum of £100 to buy a diamond ring in memory of our loving friendship'*.

But the lasting, visible effect of the legacies of Francis is to be found today in the sea-side resort of Scarborough, Yorkshire.

He created a 'Building Fund', with two sums of £20,000, which were to be invested by his trustees until required, at which time they should *'apply a competent part of the Building Fund in purchasing a piece of land at or near Scarborough in the county of York, as a site for Almshouses to be built.. and to expend a competent portion of the residue of the Building Fund in erecting upon the site purchased a suitable building, or buildings, to be called "Dr. Smarts Almshouses" for the occupation of the Upper and Middle Classes who may be in reduced circumstances and must be Protestants, and I direct that the buildings..shall be of an architecturally handsome character..and not merely as many rooms as can be erected with the money..'*.

He then created an 'Endowment Fund', with instructions that the income from this fund should be used to enlarge or improve the almshouses, or for making a *'weekly or other allowance to all or any of the Inmates thereof'*.

In a codicil he added a further sum of £20,000 to be divided between the two funds and directed the trustees to include a provision *'that the Master..of the said Almshouses shall be a properly qualified Medical Man who shall be competent to look after the health of the inmates..'*

On 25 March, 1913, just four days before she died, Marion added her fourth and final codicil to her will and included *'to my dear husband Francis Gray Smart, in loving remembrance, £20,000 free of legacy duty, and it is my hope that he will use the same for making further provision for the Dr. Smart Homes which he proposes to found'*.

I approached the present Clerk to the Trustees of Dr. Smart's Trust, Mr. William Temple, and burdened him with such questions as I thought relevant to our story and also to satisfy my own curiosity! After all, Sandra and I had been following close in the footsteps of Francis Smart for almost five years and having come so far we had to know how it all ended.

Well it actually ended very well indeed!

Mr. Temple kindly agreed to let me have sight of the first audited Accounts of the Trust.

They show that the sums of money received from the legacies were invested wisely and, with dividends and other reversionary gifts, had grown to over £112,000 by the year ending 1934. Then, having purchased the land, the talents of architect Edward Ford Duncanson were put to good use.

He was the nephew who was left the books on Architecture in the 1913 will of Francis, and those all important items '...*cameras, lenses and photographic apparatus...*'. Edward was born in 1880 and, in some respects, he followed in the footsteps of his elder brother Thomas Jones Gibb Duncanson. He, too, was educated at Harrow and Emmanuel College, Cambridge, and received his rowing 'blue' in 1901. The Great War saw him in the R.N.V.R. as a Lieutenant with the Coastal Motor Boat Service, and in 1919 he was awarded the Distinguished Service Cross. After the war he became a J.P., served on Kent County Council, and continued his career as an architect in Grays Inn Square, in the City of London, whilst living at Sundridge Avenue in Bromley, Kent. He died in 1947.

I wonder if he received the actual cameras that took the 1889 photographs; the negatives from which the prints were made and the medals Francis was awarded for them?

Perhaps he also received the 1889 album, which is now in our possession, but what has happened to all the other albums of photographs that must have graced the library shelves in Tunbridge Wells? Have any more survived?

What is surviving though, in 1991, are the *Dr. Smart Homes* in Woodlands Grove, Scarborough, that Edward Ford Duncanson designed.

They are a visual delicacy set in beautiful gardens, as I discovered when I visited the Homes, met with the gardeners and enjoyed a cup of coffee with the good humoured staff before looking around the flat of Mrs. Audrey Brown, one of the residents. The whole concept is a delight and I am certain Francis would have given his total approval to the design.

Whilst our own part of his legacy, his 1889 photograph album, is a product of his leisure time and has already given, and will continue to give, pleasure to others, the buildings in Scarborough offer much more.

Francis Smart's financial legacy has provided secure shelter in tranquil surroundings and one hopes that the trustees, present and future, will continue to provide income for the maintenance of the buildings, employment of staff and the care of the residents.

Because it was outside the scope of my research I paid no attention to the life of George Edward Smart, only brother of Francis Gray, but, however briefly, that omission must be corrected and I an indebted to Audrey Brown for pointing me in the right direction.

George Edward Smart, born in 1849, outlived all his family; he was in his ninetieth year when he died in 1939, and *his* name is also remembered in Scarborough today.

As the result of a childhood game that went wrong, George was blind in one eye and his other eye was weakened to the extent that he was unable to stand too much direct sunlight. This perhaps explains why he was considered an 'eccentric recluse' by the people of Combe Hay. But he inherited a great amount from the various estates of his late parents, brother and sister, and he carried on the traditional largess of the family.

Money was set aside for the *'Doctor Smart's Supplementary Homes'* to be built in Scarborough, although he made it clear that they should be managed independently from those of his brother.

In 1958 the 'George Edward Smart Homes' in Stepney Drive, Scarborough, were opened, the complex being named *'Combe Hay House'* in his memory. With other bequests in Yorkshire and Tunbridge Wells the Smart name, from grandfather George to grandson George Edward, continues to be remembered to this day.

The death of Marion and Francis ended this particular Smart family line, and on earth, at least, they were parted.

Marion's 1909 will opened with the words:'

'I desire to be buried in the new Cemetery at Tunbridge Wells, by the side of my late husband (Thomas Jones Gibb), and I wish my funeral to be conducted in the most simple manner and without any flowers except of the most simple kind grown in my own, or my friends, gardens'.

Written 23 years after her marriage to Francis, and still unaltered at the time of her death, these words might suggest that the union of Francis and Marion was one of convenience, following as it did so closely on the death of the first husband Thomas Jones Gibb. Be that as it may, their time on this earth was put to good use and many people were aided by their great charity and continue to receive benefit to this day. May they both Rest in Peace.

L·D·S

An idyllic corner at the 'Dr. Smart's Homes' in Scarborough, in 1990.

Photographs
From The
Album

The 'Scotch Tour 1889' Album contains 72 pages and 283 photographs. Whilst the occasional picture appears 'out of sequence' – it did not fit the correct page because of size, the photographs are pasted into the album in what we must assume was the order of the journey. This is a list of the places photographed by Francis Smart and in the order that they appear on the pages of the album:

CARLISLE, MELROSE, JEDBURGH, DRYBURGH, ABBOTSFORD, EDINBURGH;
DUNKELD, DUNBLANE, PITLOCHRY, KILLIECRANKIE, LOCH TUMMEL,
KINLOCH RANNOCH, GLEN TILT, BLAIR ATHOLL, FALLS OF BRUAR, NAIRN,
INVERNESS;
FALLS OF ROJIE, KINLOCHEWE, LOCH MAREE, LOCH TOLLIE,
POOLEWE, GAIRLOCH, AULTBEA, LOCH SHIELDAIG, BADACHRO, PORTREE;
BALMACARA, LETTERFEARN, KINTAIL, GLENELG;
EIGG, ARDNAMURCHAN, TOBERMORY, CRAIGNURE, OBAN;
LOCH AWE, TAYNUILT, DALMALLY, INVERARAY, EDINBURGH;
BERWICK, COMBE HAY, FARLEIGH CASTLE, BRADFORD ON AVON.

The selection of the illustrations used within these pages was not too difficult but it was entirely a personal choice and, with 283 originals in the album, it was decided that 123 pictures would be appropriate.

What has been omitted includes duplication of such things as the abbey buildings in the Border area, waterfalls and rivers in Perthshire, a bank of Royal Fern near Gairloch and yachts around Oban in Regatta Week. A photograph of a thatched building, however interesting to fellow members of *Cairdean nan Taighean Tugha* (Friends of the Thatched Houses), means nothing if the site cannot be identified today, and whilst the technical difficulties of recording a sunset in 1889 might delight the photographic historian, the image will not impress this generation of colour photographers, armed with those little square colour filters, who create masterpieces with each setting sun!

1   From the first page of the album, a picture taken in Carlisle by Francis Smart before he and his wife crossed the border into Scotland for their 'Scotch Tour'. But was it a market day in the city or just common grazing? Difficult to decide.

2 & 3   Two architectural studies of Jedburgh Abbey. The picture of the Norman door was exhibited, four months after it was taken, at the Tunbridge Wells Amateur Photographic Association annual exhibition and was awarded the Bronze (2nd) Medal in the Architectural Section. "The Nave is 130 feet long and has on both sides pointed arches, each one surmounted by two in the triforium and four in the clerestory. It is a pity that the fabric has required the support of a range of cross-beams." (From Baddeley's 'Thorough Guide to Scotland' 1889 Edition, the year of Francis Smart's Tour).

4   *A group of neat, unidentified cottages somewhere in the Borders area.*

5   *Melrose Abbey, described in the Baddeley's Guide of 1889 as "..a still beautiful structure..placed in a favourite route for marauding armies..it has been plundered and knocked about from motives of religion, utility, and sheer wanton robbery to such an extent that the wonder is it continues to exist at all. Open all day; moonlight nights till 11. Admission 6d."*

6   Two studies of this serving maid appear at the beginning of the album. She was photographed in the Borders area, possibly in Dryburgh, and may well have been a member of the Smart household. Her salver holds two tumblers and an engraved wine glass, all empty alas!

7   A distant view of Abbotsford, former home of Sir Walter Scott.

8   A horse drawn tram in front of number 104 Princes Street, Edinburgh, the Clarendon Hotel in 1889. Much scaffolding covers one of the buildings and all the upper deck passengers of the tram have turned to look at the work in progress.

9   A 'view from our window' reads the album caption for this Edinburgh photograph. The Turkish Baths were at number 90 Princes Street, so it is possible to place the Smart family next door at the Balmoral Hotel. Perhaps they had read, and been impressed by, the hotel advertisement at this time which proclaimed "First Class Hotel in the Principal thoroughfare, overlooking the Public Gardens and opposite the Castle. Luxuriously furnished; Cuisine superb; prices moderate; Continental languages spoken. Patronised by the Royal Family and Nobility". (Paterson's Tourist Guide to Scotland). A Littlewoods store and a branch of Body Shop occupies the site today.

10   Edinburgh Castle from West Princes Street Gardens with the ornamental fountain *"constructed at a cost of about £3000". (Shilling Handy Guide to Scotland, a contemporary guidebook).*

11   Holyrood Palace, a must for every Victorian tourist. *"Open 11am - 6pm; (Winter to 4pm). Admission 6d, Free on Saturdays..The Picture Gallery contains fanciful representations of the Scottish Monarchs from the time of Fergus I to James VII, as dull and uninteresting a collection of portraits as the eye could rest upon".* (Baddeley's Guide, 1889). *Yet another ornamental fountain, this time dominating the photograph.*

12 *Scottish soldiers photographed by Francis Smart during his stay in Edinburgh. A picture packed with little clues. They are very probably Black Watch bandsmen, for marks on the shoulders and tunic flap of the man in the centre indicate pipe clay from the straps that held the drum. The man on the right wears a bandsman's ceremonial sword and has recently returned from Egypt; his medals are the Egypt Campaign medal with one bar (probably Tel-El-Kebir) and the Khedive's Star.*

13   The Forth Rail Bridge, 100 years old in 1990 but still not linked when the Smarts visited in the summer of '89. All visitors were encouraged to see the "..works..10 minutes from South Queensferry Station with..an inn close to them. They are being pushed forward with great energy, and it is expected that the bridge will be open for traffic in 1890". (Baddeley's Guide 1889). The bridge was opened by the then Prince of Wales on March 4 1890, seven years after the work had begun.

14   Waiting for the train and an 'island platform' with a poster advertising the 1889 Paris Exhibition where visitors stared in amazement at the now famous Eiffel Tower. I hesitate to name this particular Scottish station. When this photograph was seen at the National Library of Scotland, during the centenary Winter Exhibition , the rail enthusiasts were asked to identify the station. The short-list is now down to eight names!

15   Dunblane Cathedral photographed 'from train in motion' according to the album caption. *Baddeley's Guide* in 1889 suggested that "The Cathedral here, visible from the train, will induce many visitors to halt and examine its beauties". The Smarts do not appear to have taken the hint but continued onward to Dunkeld.

16   Dunkeld and the bridge over the river Tay with the Athole Arms hotel next to the church. This latter building is now an antique emporium, but visually little has altered.

17   Dunkeld, with the fountain to the memory of George, the sixth Duke of Athole, erected in 1886. When Queen Victoria was a young girl the population of the town was over 2000, yet when this photograph was taken, 52 years into her reign, it had dropped to less than 800. The building on the left was built as a hospital in 1754. It is known as the Ell House and now serves as a shop for the National Trust for Scotland. The building to the right was granted a Civic Trust Award in 1965 although the upper right hand window has been blocked off since 1889 and a new one inserted upper left.

18   The Nave of Dunkeld Cathedral.

20   Another unnamed halt on the rail journey north towards Inverness.

19   The Black Watch Monument in Dunkeld Cathedral, below the Great East Window. Today this memorial is behind the carved screen of the altar and not readily visible to casual visitors; the colours have gone.

21   "Pitlochry has not entirely lost the rustic simplicity which it possessed before the tourists learnt to swagger and become enamoured of tables d'hote at five shillings a head....the tourist should, if possible, devote two or three days to the neighbourhood of Pitlochry". (Baddeley's Guide 1889).

22   Atholl Road, Pitlochry, looking north. The Reading Room and turreted building, known as 'Prince Charlies' House', are gone and on this spot stands a BP petrol station. Also gone are the trees and fountain; only the large building on the right remains, now a branch of the Bank of Scotland (See Page 38).

24 *A road mender 'Nr. Pitlochry'. Francis Smart wanted to record the man at his work, not posing for the camera, and it is this attention to detail that sets him apart from other less gifted amateur photographers of his day.*

23 *A young girl hurries past the camera whilst fishermen and hunter walk towards the shop of Thomas Dyer, Watchmaker and Jeweller in Pitlochry.*

26 *Captioned simply 'Tramps'. Somewhere close to Pitlochry Francis Smart came across these two women and set up his large camera, on the tripod, to record their passing. The woman with the child on her back carries an old water pail under her shawl. I have been assured that the descendants of these two travelling people still live in Pitlochry, and I have been given the same surnames from three different sources. That is too much of a coincidence to treat lightly.*

25 *Again somewhere 'Nr. Pitlochry' according to the caption, with a woman and a young girl using long rakes to gather the summer hay.*

27   The Loch Tummel Inn, just beyond Queen's View, "..a small hostelry commanding a splendid view of the water and its surroundings". (Baddeley's Guide 1889). This fine building still functions as an inn and hotel over a century later. There can be no doubt that the coachman in this photograph was in the employ of the Smart family. He was the Victorian equivalent of a chauffeur and can be seen again, serving tea at a picnic break, in Aultbea.

28   Tummel Bridge and the hotel. Today this is a much wooded area, with the photograph having been taken from what is now the site of Tummel Valley Holiday Park with 30 chalets, over 100 static caravans (with room for a further 100 tourers), pub, shop and restaurant.

29   A tranquil scene in Kinloch Rannoch with the 3550 foot high peak of Schiehallion in the background. The women wash whilst the children play on open ground. Today this land is alongside Brown's garage in the village and is not suitable for children of this age to play on. The road behind them is the main route from Tummel Bridge to Rannoch Station, but the houses of Allt Mor Crescent hide much of this 1889 view now.

30   Anxious to record in greater detail the activities of the women at Kinloch Rannoch, Francis Smart moved his camera and tripod closer. Iron pots, tin pails, wooden bowls and bundles of clothes emphasis the arduous task they undertook.

31   A stage coach at Blair Atholl, the other form of transport used by the Smarts during their tour of the Highlands.

32   An old lady at Blair Atholl, taking advantage of the long hours of summer daylight to knit stockings on her four needles. She appears to be chuckling, no doubt at the stranger with his contraption in front of her. A charming study of a woman born, undoubtedly, during the reign of George III. What changes she must have heard of, and witnessed, in her lifetime!

33   Washing day at Blair Atholl. A very familiar sight in the Highlands and one which attracted the attention of most photographers and, later, the postcard publishing trade.

34   A study of a group of unidentified people outside a house with the date stone over the door reading 'Atholl 1812'. The young child could not remain still long enough for the photographic plate to record a sharp image.

35   Quiet Glen Tilt close by Blair Atholl; 'nr. Forest Lodge' reads the caption in the album.

36   The Harbour at Nairn; the building standing alone on the horizon is a fish smoking-house, whilst the sailing boats under the harbour wall look almost ancient even at this date.

37   Nairn children with driftwood. A charming study of local children, some shy but one happy to be photographed. This picture was taken in Fishertown on the banks of the river Nairn and demonstrates Francis/Smart's great ability to compose a picture, with total strangers, and use his knowledge of the camera to obtain an informal 'formal shot' without everyone standing in line across the front of the lens.

38   *A fisherman in Nairn sorting his lines whilst the next generation looks on. Another prize winner for Francis Smart.*

39　Inverness Harbour and a peaceful place on this day. A century later, in 1989, the rail bridge which is visible, on the left of the picture, was swept away in the winter storms.

40　The entrance to the Episcopal Cathedral of St. Andrew in Inverness. It had been standing less than twenty years when Francis Smart took his picture and had been erected at a cost of some £20,000.

41　Near Inverness, and a bend in the Caledonian Canal is recorded from a popular vantage point. Edwardian postcard photographers stood on the same spot 20 years later.

42   The journey west, from Inverness through Glen Docherty and by Loch Maree, towards
Gairloch. A distinct lack of trees enabled Francis Smart to record this view but today's traveller
will not have the same good fortune as this is a much wooded area.

43   Near Kinlochewe, a peaceful spot. The very distinct features of Ben Slioch with Loch Maree in
the middle distance. Queen Victoria travelled this route in 1877 and stayed six nights in the local
hotel .

44   *A group of dwellings on the west coast at Aultbea, a lonely spot in the 1880s.*

45   *A private family picnic at Aultbea and Marion Smart can now be positively identified as the seated lady in this picture. She also appears on the steps of her father in law's house in Combe Hay, Bath, with him by her side. The chance discovery of a small book in Tunbridge Wells library, which contained a photograph of Marion Smart, led to her identification here. The servant has already been photographed outside the hotel at Loch Tummel in the driver's seat of a coach and, with the lady's maid, is one of at least twelve persons employed by the family at this time.*

46   Children gathering whelks at Aultbea. Sit and have a coffee in the restaurant of the Aultbea Hotel today and look out beyond the car park wall to the shore itself. These children stood just about 100 yards away in 1889 when Francis Smart negotiated the wet rocks with his cumbersome camera and tripod.

47   Below the bridge at Poolewe the women do their washing and today, a century later, this site is virtually unchanged. In November 1889 Francis Smart exhibited this photograph at the Tunbridge Wells Amateur Photographic Association annual exhibition. It won the 'Amateur Photographer' magazine Bronze Medal, presented by the editor Charles W. Hastings, and the Silver (1st) Medal in the Genre Section of the competition.

48   A grand panorama showing the village of Poolewe which "...consists chiefly of a long row of houses, terminated seawards by a very comfortable little inn. The Glasgow steamer calls once a fortnight. There is nothing calling for remark in the place itself". (Baddeley's Guide to the Northern Highlands, 1885 edition). The large house, on the right and in the distance, was home to a Mr. Osgood Mackenzie at this time. It is standing in the grounds of Inverewe Gardens, which he created, and which now belong to the National Trust for Scotland.

49   A photograph taken from a window at the Gairloch Hotel, yet another stopping place for the family at "..a first class hotel, under new management". (Baddeley's Guide 1889).

50   The morning coach loading at the Gairloch Hotel. Just as today this was a busy hotel for the coach trade with connections to the Highland Railway station at Achnasheen some 28 miles away. The coach journey in 1889 took five hours at a cost of 9/- (45p).

51   A panoramic view near Gairloch with Loch Tollie in the foreground.

52   Away from Gairloch and a moment of peace at Badachro. The tranquillity can only be *imagined. There would be no sound of motor vehicles, radios or high flying transatlantic jets. Just total peace. What amazing changes Francis Smart was to witness during the next twenty four years until his death in 1913.*

53   *A little corner of Loch Shieldaig near Gairloch.*

54   Portree Harbour from the deck of the paddle steamer 'Mountaineer' en route from Gairloch to Oban. Arrival time at Portree, during the summer of 1889, was between 7 and 7.30 a.m. but this hardly justifies the total absence of people on shore. Under the large tree is a small stone building which in 1889 was the Portree commercial ice-house supplying the fishing vessels in the harbour.

55   Onwards from Portree towards Balmacara and Glenelg and through Kyle, with the lighthouse and the ruin of Caisteal Maol at Kyleakin.

56   The lighthouse on Eilean Ban (the Fair Island), lying in the narrows between Kyle and Kyleakin, the present, regular, crossing point between the mainland and Skye.

57   Returning to the steamer after spending time ashore at Balmacara. This picture shows Balmacara House with a private steam yacht in the bay.

58   In this picture taken at Balmacara the larger building, centre, served as a waiting room for David MacBrayne's ferry-boat passengers in 1889. Today it belongs to the National Trust for Scotland, is known as Ferry Cottage, and is available to members as a holiday letting cottage. Join now and put your name on the waiting list!

59   A fine thatched building doing duty as a licensed grocery for M. Grant, and serving the people of Kintail as their Post Office in 1889. Of this building today nothing remains. A bus shelter and a telephone box opposite Shiel Bridge marks the site now.

60   Letterfearn on the road around Loch Duich towards Totaig, and Francis Smart photographs a local woman with her baskets whilst in the coach, in the background, his wife Marion sits watching and waiting.

61 An upturned hulk at Letterfearn with the village in the background. The net drying poles still exist to this day but the trees appear to be fewer in number now. The old school building, now converted into a house, is visible just above the left end of the boat.

62 Along the shore of Loch Duich at Letterfearn. It is still possible to recognize this area today as little has changed. In front of the principal building in the photograph there is a corrugated shed today, although the thatched dwelling still remains.

63 A landing stage at Letterfearn; the opposite shore now carries the main A87 road through Inverinate to Kyle of Lochalsh and the ferry crossing to Skye. Boats still use this landing-place.

94

64   A much photographed scene, the Clachan at Letterfearn. Just beyond the public phone box, with the telephone number Dornie 256, is the site of this picture but do not expect to see the cottages with their neat thatch today. Accept this photograph as one of the best records of the past as you will hardly recognize the immediate area now. In front of the door of the cottage is an upturned box with a pestle and mortar; It was used for crushing bait for the fishing.

65   More crofts in Letterfearn, probably near Croit na h-Abaid. The left-hand building was a barn and the one with the pointed roof appears to have an outer wooden cover at the side which may have housed a water wheel.

95

66   An evocative study of children in Letterfearn. The composition reflects the late Victorian trend
of creating with the camera what the artist did with brush and canvas. This is quite a superb
picture by Francis Smart and a personal favourite. Every effort has been made to identify some of
these children but no positive names have been put to faces as yet. No doubt a MacRae, or a Forbes
or two!

67   Peaceful and remote Glenelg. After the
bustle of Edinburgh, the commerce of Pitlochry
and the sophistication of Inverness, the
opportunity to stay in Glenelg was, and still is,
a great relief to the visitor. This is a view
across the river looking towards Galtair and
the road to the ferry across to Kylerhea, Isle of
Skye.

68   A small corner of Galtair, Glenelg, with
thatched crofts nestling under the cliff.

69   Across the river looking towards the houses of Galtair, Glenelg.

70   The drove road leading away from Kylerhea, and Skye, through Galtair. This was the main route for the drovers coming from Skye and the Outer Isles, heading for the markets in the south, such as Falkirk.

71   Galtair, Glenelg, showing the track down to Riverfoot.

72   A boat passing through the narrows at Kylerhea ferry. The far shore is the island of Skye.

73   A group of crofts at Riverfoot, Glenelg.

74   A place long known as Market Stance, Glenelg. Fairs or markets were held in Glenelg on all Fridays after the last Tuesday of May and on the third Tuesdays of August and September. (Ordnance Gazetteer of Scotland, Vol.III, 1895).

75   Looking towards Glen Beag, Glenelg.

76   The camp of a travelling family of tinsmiths, or tinkers, at Market Stance, Galtair, Glenelg. Modern caravans park on this exact spot today, their owners probably unaware of the little piece of history attached to this site. Little else has changed, although a modern bungalow has been built less than fifty yards away to the right. The trees still survive as do both walls, despite the many gaps which are now appearing in the front wall. The young girl on the right, peeping around the tent, appears on the front cover of this book with her elder sister, Isabella.

100

77   *The summer of 1889 in Glenelg and everyone helps to bring in the harvest. Of the sixteen people who appear on the original negative, the front group of five reap the crop with scythes whilst the rear team gather, bind and stack. Only the little boy seems to have noticed Francis Smart and his camera. I bet he told all his friends about it later!*

78　*More harvesting in Glenelg but now everyone has stopped work and posed in front of the camera lens.*

79　*Crofts in Galtair, Glenelg. The house on the left was the home of the MacLeod family at this time; mother, father and three children. A fourth child, Flora, was born in this house at 3 p.m. on the afternoon of 3 January, 1890.*

80   A simple but well posed photograph of a family on their croft in Galtair, Glenelg, on an August day in 1889. The bare facts but, with the exception of the man on the extreme right, we now know a great deal about these people. The centre figure and head of the household is John MacLeod (Iain Mor), a 47 year old shoemaker and son of Angus (a shepherd) and Flora (nee Campbell). In December 1880 John was on the island of North Uist for his wedding to 29 year old Mary Matheson of Malaclete, daughter of Donald and Anne (nee MacAskill). In descending order the children in the picture, with their mother, are Mary Ann (better known as Kate in later life), born June, 1883; Angus, born April, 1886, who died in Campbeltown in the late 1970s, and Donald the baby, born February, 1888, who was eventually to emigrate to New Zealand. All the children were born in Glenelg. Their mother Mary is quite obviously pregnant and on 3 January, 1890, she gave birth to Flora who is especially remembered in Glenelg for her skill as a tram driver in Glasgow during World War I. The eldest girl, Mary Ann (Ceit Iain Mhoir), lived and died in Galtair, Glenelg, retaining the croft after the death of her parents. Francis Smart also photographed the family home during his 1889 tour (79).

81   A house in the main street of Glenelg. In fact the last house in the street as you pass the present day Post Office towards the Glenelg Inn. Sweet jars and other such items fill the window so it is possible to assume that it was a shop in 1889. Records show that Catherine Morrison, a single lady from Inverness, was the shopkeeper in the village at this time. Might this be her?

82   *The holiday accommodation of the Smart family whilst in Glenelg.*

"This Hotel, which has been rebuilt, is situated in one of the most beautiful parts of the West Coast of Scotland, easy of access by daily steamer from Oban and quite near the island of Skye. The scenery all round is magnificent.

The Hotel is one of the most comfortable in the North of Scotland, and is under the personal supervision of the lessee, Donald MacDonald MacKintosh.

The bedrooms are large, airy and comfortable and the Coffee Room affords excellent accommodation. The Cooking is good, and the Wines and Spirits have been selected with great care. Gentlemen staying at GLENELG HOTEL have the privilege of SALMON and SEA-TROUT FISHING FREE on the Glenelg River; also GROUSE, BLACK GAME and HARE SHOOTING by the week or month at a Moderate Charge. The Sea Fishing is about the best on the West Coast.

BOATS AND BOATMEN. BILLIARDS. HOT, COLD AND SHOWER BATHS.

Among places of interest near are the Pictish Towers of Glenbeg, Cup Marked Stones, Glenbeg Water Falls, Loch Duich, Loch Hourn, Glenshiel, Falls of Glomach, Shiel Hotel, Ec.." (Glenelg Hotel advertisement for the 1889 season). On a Sunday evening in March, 1947, a fire broke out on the premises and, despite the very gallant efforts of the villagers, the hotel was destroyed.

83 A view in Glenelg showing "The Bernera Barracks, a little way north (of the hotel) and now in ruins...another reminder of the difficulties which the present dynasty at first experienced with the Highland clans". (Baddeley's Guide 1889).

84 In Cosaig, Glenelg. A croft known as Redburn in which lived Aonghas Ban (Fair Angus because of the colour of his hair), and his two sisters Kirsty and Mary MacLean. Glenelg is still home to at least two great-grand nieces of this family.

85   *More of the dwellings in Cosaig, Glenelg; the houses in the main street lie to the right of the picture.*

86   *The Glenelg Highland Games of 1889. A unique record of this village gathering which gave everyone a lot of fun and provided plenty of material for Francis Smart and his cameras. The field of combat, for anyone following the '89 Tour today, is on the left, behind and below the old Manse House, just before you enter Glenelg village itself.*

The piper is reputed to be David Mather, composer of 'Loch Carron' amongst other pipe tunes. He was footman to the Master of Blantyre, the Hon. Walter Stuart, who owned Eileanreach House some three miles away. He died in Montana in the United States of America in 1943.

87   The Champion of Glenelg, said to be a man named Ali Mor.

88   The Tug of War. At least two uniformed police officers can be seen in this photograph so the Constabulary had provided the local officer, North Uist man Alexander MacVicar, with extra help for the day! The ladies are holding parasols rather than umbrellas and the ground is obviously mud-free. Visibility appears to be excellent and the good weather has brought out the crowds.

89   Tossing the Caber. The man astride the horse, immediately behind the competitor, is probably the judge for this particular event.

90   *And over it goes! Or did it?*

91   *Dancing the Reel. Photographed on a hand-held, quarter plate, camera, Francis Smart has captured in this picture a view of his main camera on the very right hand edge of the negative; a half plate field camera on tripod. It cannot be doubted that this is his own camera unless other, as yet unknown, images of these 1889 Games come to light. No known photographs of games in Glenelg at this time have been located in any public collections in Scotland.*

110

92   The High Jump. The tall bearded man standing by the upright has been named as one Duncan Gillies by two independent sources.

93   *The Sack Race. A quarter plate image taken with a hand-held camera which allowed the Victorian photographer greater mobility than he had previously experienced.*

The men were actually sewn into the wool sacks, no doubt to stop illegal tactics! This picture gave the final clue to the identification of Francis Gray Smart as the photographer. In the Winter Exhibition Catalogue, 1892, of the Tunbridge Wells Amateur Photographic Association, Francis Smart is shown as having submitted prints in Class VIII "from negatives taken with a Hand Camera". His entries were titled 'Tossing the Caber' and 'Sack Race'. (Catalogue of the 6th Annual Exhibition of the Tunbridge Wells Amateur Photographic Association; held November 1892 in the Royal Sussex Assembly Rooms, Tunbridge Wells, and opened by the President himself, Francis Gray Smart. [Catalogue in the Tunbridge Wells Library]).

With the permission of the MacPherson family I have included their picture of Jessie MacLean as she looked some 30 years after being photographed by Francis Smart.

94   Crofting woman at Quarry, Glenelg. As the manuscript of this book was going from publisher to printer I received a letter from a friend in Glenelg, Margaret MacPherson. I had asked Margaret to look at all of Francis Smart's photographs of the area, check my locations and Gaelic spelling, and make any corrections or comments. Referring to the houses in Quarry (95-97), but not having seen the list of inhabitants, she wrote "..the last house was occupied by my great grandparents John MacLean and Jessie his wife...". This confirmed the research notes in my possession,but what I did not expect was the next paragraph in Margaret's letter.."As my mother was looking through the photographs she recognised the strange curly hair and the nose (of the lady) in this picture. It was taken just along from her house in Quarry and is undoubtedly my great grandmother Jessie MacLean. My mother (having got home) has sent me the only photo she has of her grandmother, taken when she was much older - in her seventies in the 1920s - and there is no doubt, by the expression of the eyes and eyebrows, nose and hair, that it is the same woman."

95-97   *Leading away from the village of Glenelg proper, a group of four houses lay beyond the hotel, and the pier which is close to the present day War Memorial, to an area known as Quarry. All of the houses appear on these photographs and it is possible to name the occupants of them in the month of August 1889 when the pictures were being taken. The last house on the right, with the two chimneys, was the home of boat builder John MacLean, his wife Jessie and children Ann, Hector, Finlay and Murdoch aged between 14 and 6 years. Next door, in the long low thatched dwelling, lived boatman Alexander MacLeod with his wife Mary and son Murdoch. Their neighbours were Alexander MacRae, and his children Sarah and Donald. The first house, nearest to Glenelg village, was the home of Ewen and Isabella MacIntyre; all the inhabitants of Quarry in 1889.*

98   A Tinker Woman in Glenelg. Now nationally acclaimed to be the finest picture ever taken of a travelling tinsmith, this single photograph receives the greatest comment, praise and admiration whenever it is seen. It was chosen for the poster and leaflet in the National Library of Scotland Winter Exhibition of 1989, and with television and press coverage it must have been seen by more people than Francis Smart could ever have imagined. The young girl on the left is 9 year old Henrietta Stewart and she is standing alongside her married sister, 24 year old Isabella MacDonald. On Isabella's back is her son Solomon, born in April 1889. They are stood outside the home of Alexander MacLeod in Quarry (95-97) with the gable end of Jessie MacLean's house showing on the right (94 shows Jessie herself). More details of the Stewart family appear elsewhere in this book.

99   The 'Pictish Tower' at Glenbeag, near Glenelg, better known as Dun Troddan. The tree has survived the past 100 years but a wooden gate now marks the entrance to this ancient broch.

100-1   Waiting for the Steamer, Glenelg, at "...the little stone pier, to which passengers are conveyed to and from the steamers in commodious boats.." (Baddeley's Guide 1889). An exposed place especially during inclement weather. The hotel guests however could watch, from the comfort of the lounge, the steamer coming through the narrows at Kylerhea and still have time to walk to the pier before the boats came ashore.

102 *Below the jetty, Glenelg. Tied up at the pier is one of Mr. MacBrayne's smaller boats.*

103 *David MacBrayne's paddle steamer 'Mountaineer' off Glenelg and bound for Oban. In 1889 the advertised schedule for this vessel was: Oban-Craignure-Lochaline-Salen-Tobermory-Arisaig-Armadale-Glenelg-Balmacara-Kyleakin-Broadford-Portree-Gairloch, departing Tuesday, Thursday and Saturday at a cost of 25/- for Cabin passengers and 15/- Steerage Class; time on voyage 13.5 hours. On Monday, Wednesday and Friday she returned from Gairloch, departing from Glenelg at 11 a.m. for arrival in Oban at 5.50 p.m. This photograph of the 'Mountaineer', in early September 1889, may be one of the last ever taken. Heading from Glenelg to Oban on 27 September she ran aground in bad weather near the Lismore light. All the passengers and crew were rescued but salvage work was delayed because of storms and by early October she had broken up and sunk. A sad end indeed. (See 'West Highland Steamers' by Messrs. Duckworth and Langmuir. All you want to know about the ships of the West Highlands and Islands will be there; various editions from 1935 onward but the third of 1967 is my choice).*

104 On board the 'Mountaineer' and bound for Oban. A fine day with time to admire the view and chat to fellow passengers before lunch.

105   The Scuir of Eigg - a very distinctive feature on the journey south from Glenelg to Oban.

106   The shore-line of Tobermory, Isle of Mull, photographed with a hand-held camera from the deck of the inward bound paddle steamer.

107 *Passengers boarding at Craignure, Isle of Mull.*

108 *Oban at last and the Smarts have a good view from the window at their hotel, in 1889 called The Station Hotel but now renamed Caledonian Hotel. The line of buildings running from left to centre has hardly changed in over 100 years but the same cannot be said for those in George Street, running from the right towards the centre of the picture. For all the long suffering residents of Oban here is a picture of the town before the motor car arrived. The urgent need, as we approach the 21st century, is for space for the people and somewhere else to park the car away from this part of town.*

109 *A corner of Oban Bay with nets drying in the foreground and a small boat, OB 1, lying close to the pier.*

110 *"The following yachts were in the bay during the week: Columba, s.s., Duke of Argyll: Alca, s s., Colonel Malcolm of Poltalloch, M.P.: Lyra, s.s., Sir William Brown: Black Pearl, s.s., Earl of Pembroke: Bessie, s.s., T. Sopwith of Kilchearan, Lismore and London: Cressida, s.s., Earl of Morton, etc.. " (Oban Times, 14 September, 1889, where a more complete list can be found).*

111 *Thursday 12 September 1889 the day of the Royal Highland Yacht Club Regatta. The 'Oban Times' observed "The morning was dull and hazy. There was a dead calm and the prospects for the regatta were not encouraging, with the clouds lying low on the hills...the bay was crowded with a fine fleet of steam yachts ...all the yachts got up their bunting and the bay presented a very pretty appearance..."*

112 *The paddle steamer 'Pioneer' at the North Pier, Oban. Already 45 years old when this photograph was taken, she continued in service until 1895. Her regular run at this time was from Oban through the Sound of Mull.*

113-15   The Argyllshire Gathering and Games, Oban, Wednesday 11 September 1889. "The weather, though sometimes threatening, continued fair, and the different events passed off very successfully. Throughout the entire day the behaviour of the large crowds was most exemplary, and though as usual additional police had been drafted into the town from outlying districts..it is gratifying to state that their assistance was never required to any appreciable extent." (Oban Times, 14 September 1889).

116 A family group at Taynuilt. This building, much altered and enlarged, is a very popular village sweet shop today.

117 A herd of cattle at Dalmally. No doubt Francis photographed the beasts with his own father in mind; Dr. John Smart bred Jersey cows.

118 A view captioned 'From our window Loch Awe Hotel'. Further evidence that Francis and Marion Smart enjoyed an unhurried holiday with frequent halts at some of the best hotels.

119 Inveraray Harbour. One of the last photographs taken by Francis Smart during his extensive 'Scotch Tour' of 1889.

120 *Waverley Station, Edinburgh. The holiday is over and only the final train journey to England remains.*

121 At Combe Hay. A herd of Jersey cattle owned and tended by Dr. John Smart, the father of Francis.

122-3   And finally, two photographs from the last pages of the album. They are captioned 'Combe Hay', a small village near Bath, in England. Their inclusion in the album was vital to the identification of Francis Gray Smart as the photographer on the 'Scotch Tour 1889'. On the steps of the Manor House stands Marion, wife of Francis Gray Smart, with her father in law, and former physician from Tunbridge Wells, Dr. John Cass Smart who had retired a few years earlier.